WRITERS AND CRITICS

Chief Editor

A. NORMAN JEFFARES

Advisory Editors

DAVID DAICHES

C. P. SNOW

The subject of this book is too rare a bird to be pigeon-holed. Many reviewers of Hugh MacDiarmid's *Collected Poems*, while impressed by the formidable range and variety of his work, found him very difficult to place, being much too far north of London and east of New York. For the general reader, then, a certain amount of difficulty in coming to terms with the work is to be expected.

Kenneth Buthlay has made use of a great deal of little-known material in clarifying the nature of the particular problems involved, so as to help new readers to an understanding of what exactly MacDiarmid has tried to do and to what extent he has succeeded in doing it. Writing from Brazil, where he is in charge of the English Department at the University of São Paulo, Professor Buthlay has the unusual advantage of being out of touch with fashionable literary circles. While well aware of the unevenness of MacDiarmid's work, he communicates something of the exhilarating unpredictability, the verbal agility, sleight-of-mind, and speculative stamina that give so much sheer pleasure when the poet is at his best. And at his best there is only one word for MacDiarmid: great.

HUGH MACDIARMID
(C. M. GRIEVE)

KENNETH BUTHLAY

OLIVER AND BOYD
EDINBURGH AND LONDON

OLIVER AND BOYD LTD
Tweeddale Court
Edinburgh 1

39A Welbeck Street
London W.1

First published 1964

Printed in Great Britain for Oliver and Boyd Ltd
by Robert MacLehose and Co. Ltd, Glasgow

CONTENTS

ACKNOWLEDGMENTS

For permission to quote from the works of Hugh MacDiarmid, acknowledgments are due to Dr C. M. Grieve, the *Glasgow Herald*, the Macmillan Company, and Methuen & Co. Ltd.

Acknowledgment is also due to the *Glasgow Herald* for permission to quote from Edwin Morgan, "Hugh MacDiarmid: The Poet at Seventy."

The photograph on the front cover is reproduced by permission of Michael Peto.

Amongst those who have been helpful by sending me copies of some of the rarest items in the MacDiarmid bibliography, my thanks are due especially to Miss Eloah Giocomelli, Mrs Lydia Simpson of the *Glasgow Herald* library, and Mrs James Sandoe, acquisitions librarian at the University of Colorado.

K.B.

ABBREVIATED TITLES
BY WHICH THE WORKS OF
HUGH MACDIARMID AND PERIODICALS
ARE CITED IN REFERENCES

References in brackets are to *Collected Poems*.

A.	=	*Annals of the Five Senses.*
Alb.	=	*Albyn, or Scotland and the Future.*
A.S.T.	=	*At the Sign of the Thistle.*
B.C.	=	*The Burns Chronicle.*
C.C.	=	*The Circumjack Cencrastus.*
C.P.	=	*Collected Poems.*
C.S.S.	=	*Contemporary Scottish Studies.*
D.M.	=	*A Drunk Man Looks at the Thistle* (1956).
D.R.	=	*The Daily Record and Mail.*
E.	=	*The Evergreen.*
1st H.	=	*First Hymn to Lenin and Other Poems.*
F.G.S.	=	*Francis George Scott: An Essay.*
F.M.	=	*The Free Man.*
G.H.	=	*The Glasgow Herald.*
G.T.	=	*The Golden Treasury of Scottish Poetry.*
I.M.J.J.	=	*In Memoriam James Joyce.*
K.P.W.	=	*The Kind of Poetry I Want.*
K.W.	=	*A Kist of Whistles.*
L.P.	=	*Lucky Poet.*
M.S.	=	*The Modern Scot.*
N.A.	=	*The New Age.*
N.N.	=	*Northern Numbers.*
N.R.	=	*The Northern Review.*
P.W.	=	*Penny Wheep.*
R.A.	=	*Revue Anglo-Americaine.*
S.	=	*Sangschaw.*
S.C.	=	*The Scottish Chapbook.*
S.E.J.	=	*The Scottish Educational Journal.*
2nd H.	=	*Second Hymn to Lenin* (1932).
2nd H. & O.	=	*Second Hymn to Lenin and Other Poems* (1935).
S.L.	=	*Stony Limits and Other Poems.*
S.L.S.U.	=	*Stony Limits and Scots Unbound and Other Poems.*
S.M.	=	*The Scots Magazine.*
S.N.	=	*The Scottish Nation.*
S.O.	=	*The Scots Observer.*
S.P.	=	*Selected Poems.*
S.R.	=	*The Saltire Review.*
S.Sc.	=	*Scottish Scene.*
S.U.	=	*Scots Unbound and Other Poems.*
T.L.S.	=	*The Times Literary Supplement.*
V. of S.	=	*The Voice of Scotland.*

CHAPTER I

INTRODUCTORY

The name "Hugh MacDiarmid" is more of a *nom de guerre* than a *nom de plume*. The Philistinism of modern Scotland has driven a very large number of her writers into pseudonymity, but Hugh MacDiarmid is the scourge of the Philistines, the ruthless intellectual tough looking for a rumble, the catapulted stone amongst the stool pigeons. Not for him the prolonged agony, in the words of Kierkegaard, of "being trampled to death by geese."[1]

It is strange to think of him as the inseparable companion of Christopher Murray Grieve, a peaceable, kindly, generous, and tolerant person, now more than seventy years old, devoted to the disinterested pursuit of imaginative thought and leading a quiet, rustic, ascetic life—except when on occasion he is lured to some city by riotous acquaintances (including, no doubt, MacDiarmid). Near Biggar, in Lanarkshire, there is a very simple, two-roomed cottage, and, at the back of this, a mysterious sort of hut. The latter is a secret arsenal where formidable stocks of weapons and ammunition are concealed by MacDiarmid in the books, periodicals and clippings he has amassed over the years. In the cottage itself is to be found Christopher Grieve, contemplating "how miraculously things contrary one to another concurre to the beautie and perfection of this Universe,"[2] applying himself to the Golden Rule of *Fidelity in Small Things*,[3] or quietly entertaining a few of his younger friends "like a kind, avuncular teddy bear."[4]

The vital part of Grieve's life cannot be separated from his works, the great majority of which have been written

under the name of MacDiarmid. The bare facts are
simple enough. He was born in Langholm, near the
Scottish-English border, on 11 Aug. 1892. His father was
a rural postman, active in the affairs of the Church, who
in his later years did "a great deal locally for the Co-
operative and Trade Union movements."[5] Grieve himself places great importance on the fact that he had

> a class-conscious upbringing which conditioned but did
> not distort my view of life. My development owed a
> very great deal to my growing up in a working-class
> family and being fed on out-and-out Radicalism and
> Republicanism when still a child.[6]

Of broader significance was the happy accident that the
Langholm Public Library was housed in the same building as the Grieve family. He had free access to a collection
of "upwards of twelve thousand books" and by his own
account had "certainly read almost every one of them"
by the time he left home for Edinburgh at the age of
fourteen.[7]

Such difficulties as came about between the adolescent
boy and his family seem to have centred on the "ambitious
gentility" of his mother,[8] and the opposition of both
parents to his early decision to become a poet. His break
with their devout religion appears to have been accomplished with the minimum of recrimination, perhaps because (as his work shows) he retained a deep awareness
of religious issues while rejecting all the orthodoxies.

He went to school at Langholm Academy and had the
good fortune of being taught English first by the song-
composer, F. G. Scott, on whom he was to rely heavily
for understanding and criticism of his earlier poetry, and
then by an excellent scholar, William Burt. His head-
master told the boy's father that there was a "terrible
vein of recklessness" in him, concealed behind the
deceptively quiet exterior, but added that Christopher
was the one of the two sons that "really mattered"—if he

did not "spoil it all by sheer carelessness."[9] (This anecdote is recounted by MacDiarmid in his autobiography, *Lucky Poet*—one of the most careless books ever published by a serious writer.)

He was again lucky in his English-teacher, George Ogilvie, at Broughton Junior Student Centre in Edinburgh. But the most decisive influence of all may have come from an unnamed person, about whom readers of some of his work may well have mixed feelings, and of whom he has said:

In my early teens
I had a friend who taught me to remember everything.[10]

Although Grieve qualified this to read, "I mean everything about Scotland, of course," the rider must have been added in a weak moment when he was forgetful of the quotation from Margery Allingham which heads *Lucky Poet*: "The main thing to remember in autobiography, I have always thought, is not to let any damned modesty creep in to spoil the story."[11]

His father's death in 1911 released him from what appears to have been the mere formality of training as a teacher in Edinburgh. He had already joined the Independent Labour Party (at the age of sixteen), and was a member of various local Socialist societies. In 1912 he became a journalist, working for a number of newspapers in Scotland, and also near the Welsh-English border, where he was in close contact with Keir Hardie. The research which he carried out for a Fabian Committee on Land Problems and Rural Development was used and duly acknowledged in a book on *The Rural Problem* published by Constable for the Fabian Research Department in the following year.[12] He also had his first offering to Orage's *New Age* accepted—"and I thought I had achieved world-wide fame!"[13]

In 1915 he joined the R.A.M.C. and served in Salonika, Italy, and France. Although he never saw ser-

vice on the Western Front, a devastating and terrifying
account of a soldier's feelings during the Battle of Loos,
" 'Twas in September" by "Quintus Decimus,"[14] seems
almost certain to be his work.

He married Margaret Skinner in June 1918, when
invalided home from Salonika with cerebral malaria, but
was not demobilised until 1920. The couple then settled
in Montrose, where two children were born, and the poet
earned his living as general factotum for the *Montrose
Review*. He remained there, apart from a brief expedition
to the Highlands, until 1929, becoming a Labour member of the Town Council, a J.P., and the greatest literary
force in Scotland. He was one of the founders of the
Scottish Centre of P.E.N. (1927) and the National Party
of Scotland (1928), but his subsequent relations with both
these bodies were stormy, to say the least. He also
founded, and edited, a number of periodicals with the
aim of furthering a "Scottish Renaissance Movement"
which was largely his own creation, and his break with
the Movement in 1939, when he opted for "Scottish
Workers' Republicanism à la John Maclean,"[15] was more
apparent than real.

In 1928 he was the guest of the Irish nation at the Taill-
tean Games in Dublin and made personal contacts with
the leaders of the Irish literary movement. The following
year, he went to London at the invitation of Compton
Mackenzie to work on *Vox*, a magazine connected with
the new medium of radio, which was expected to follow
up Mackenzie's success with *The Gramophone*. *Vox* fell on
deaf ears, and acute domestic troubles followed.

His experiences in England were far from happy—a
fact that may cast some light on the increasing bitterness
of his Anglophobia—but what concerns his private life is
of course no one's business but his own. He has made two
specific statements about this period: "After . . . one most
unfortunate interlude in London, and a subsequent year
in Liverpool (equally unfortunate, but for other and far

more painful reasons, and owing perhaps to a considerable extent to my own blame), I have been desperately anxious not to leave Scotland again." And "My story . . . is the story of an absolutist whose absolutes came to grief in his private life."[16]

In Liverpool, in 1930, he worked as a public relations officer with the Organisation for Advancing the Interests of Merseyside. In London again, a little later, he joined a publishing firm, the Unicorn Press.

He was divorced in January 1932, and subsequently married Valda Trevlyn, by whom he has a son, Michael, also a journalist. By the end of 1932 he was describing himself in print as a Communist,[17] though he did not join the Party until 1934, when his decision to do so caused considerable perturbation amongst the more doctrinaire members. After much trouble with the Scottish Nationalists because of his Communism, and with the Communists because of his Nationalism, he was expelled from the C.P. in 1938. He did not rejoin it until 1957—precisely when so many members were leaving it because of the Hungarian Uprising. He said on that occasion that he saw no reason to throw out the Communist baby along with the humanitarian bathwater; to which should be added his earlier statement that

. . . I am like Zamyatin. I must be a Bolshevik
Before the Revolution, but I'll cease to be one quick
When Communism comes to rule the roost.[18]

Another cause of friction with the Party was his passionate belief in C. H. Douglas's Social Credit scheme. In "the dialectics of a changing situation" until "the achievement of an integrated Communism," he still believes that recourse should be had to Douglas economics.[19] But then Communism itself is for him "a stage on the way to Anarchism," albeit "a necessary and indispensable stage."[20]

In 1933 he moved with his family to Whalsay, in the

Shetland Islands. Dr David Orr has given a moving account of the extreme hardships they endured, the break-
down in his health, the magnificent "singleness of spirit,
strength of mind and courage of heart—the essence of
MacDiarmid"—that survived it all. "There was little
food in his house, yet he ate; no water, still he drank and
washed; while his home was a cottar's house, in which the
isle's folk refused to live, as a previous dweller had died of
an infectious disease."[21] Worst of all, for him, was being
cut off from his books, his supply of periodicals, and the
stimulating friction of mind against mind. Yet he gave
his autobiography the title *Lucky Poet*.

He remained in Whalsay until 1941, when he took a
war job involving heavy manual labour in a Clydeside
factory. From this he moved to the Merchant Service and
worked on ships engaged in estuarial duties till the end of
the War. He was then fifty-three years old.

After two years in Glasgow and a subsequent spell near
Strathaven, he moved in 1951 to the little cottage a few
miles from Biggar where he still lives. Since 1949 he has
travelled extensively behind the Iron Curtain. He was
awarded a Civil List pension in 1950 and an honorary
LL.D. from Edinburgh University in 1957—remarkable
trophies for a man who has always devoted a large part of
his time to an unholy war against the vested interests of
the Anglo-Scottish Establishment, together with

the whole gang of high mucky-mucks, famous fatheads,
old wives of both sexes, stuffed shirts, hollow men with
headpieces stuffed with straw, bird-wits, lookers-under-
beds, trained seals, creeping Jesuses, Scots Wha Ha'e-
vers, village idiots, policemen, leaders of white-mouse
factions and noted connoisseurs of bread and butter,
glorified gangsters, and what 'Billy' Phelps calls
Medlar Novelists (the medlar being a fruit that becomes rotten before it is ripe), Commercial Calvinists,
makers of 'noises like a turnip', and all the touts and

toadies and lickspittles of the English Ascendancy, and their infernal women-folk, and all their skunkoil skulduggery.[22]

As may have been gathered from the above, much of MacDiarmid's prose is polemical. Comparatively little of it has found its way into books, as distinct from periodicals or pamphlets, and little space will be given to it in this study—with regret, but of necessity. However, perhaps his greatest triumph has been achieved, not because of his polemical prose campaigns for a revival of the Scots language, but rather because of the use to which he put that language in his own verse.

Nowadays in Scotland, when a young poet begins to write, he is at least aware of Scots or "Lallans" (or "the Doric," as it used to be called not so long ago) as a language in which he might choose to write his verse rather than in English. Gaelic offers another possibility, of course, for a very few: but the fact that Scots has a respectable status as a medium for serious poetry is very largely due to MacDiarmid. When he himself as an extremely ambitious but still green poet first considered the possibilities of Scots as a literary medium more than forty years ago, he shared the general opinion that nothing substantial could be achieved. Since the time of Robert Burns, verse in Scots had sunk to a level beneath serious consideration, and the few exceptions to the general rule promised little or nothing beyond their own limited achievement. An educated man might write Scots verse (or Latin verse) as an exercise. Or he might use it for convivial or amorous ditties. Or—and this most frequently—he might use its narrow channel to drain off excess sentiment and nostalgia for the lost simplicities of childhood—his own and that of his nation. But it was, generally speaking, no more promising as an art medium than the "dialect fiction" of the Kailyard School of Novelists which had been presided over by "Ian Maclaren," S. R.

Crockett, and (before he turned his attentions elsewhere) J. M. Barrie. Regarding the produce of the Kailyard, MacDiarmid was just one of many Scotsmen who strongly resented that "base caricature of their countrymen, paving the way for the grosser tradition of Lauderism."[23]

But what especially angered, and thus interested, MacDiarmid was the endless rehashing of Burns, and the fulsome lip-service paid to his genius by people who had little but contempt for poetry in every other respect, and not even the rudiments of standards by which to judge it. The Burns Cult offered a glorious opportunity for satire, an opportunity of which MacDiarmid has availed himself several times. The best of all his squibs is the story which appears in his prose collection *At the Sign of the Thistle* (1934), a volume which also contains a vigorous essay on Burnsian Bardolatory. His latest word on the subject—and several other subjects as well—is to be found in *Burns Today and Tomorrow* (1959).

Ironically enough, it was the early activities of the Vernacular Circle of the London Burns Club, founded in 1920, that focused MacDiarmid's interest on the language and literature of his own country. The Circle arranged lectures by a number of experts, including a particularly interesting one on "The Present State of the Scottish Tongue"[24] by W. A. Craigie, then Professor of Anglo-Saxon at Oxford. In this lecture, delivered on 10 Jan. 1921, Craigie clarified the possibility of a revival of Scots as a national language by citing fairly recent examples of the successful resuscitation of many languages that had been widely regarded as moribund. These included Frisian, Catalan, Provençal, Breton, Bohemian, Hungarian, Flemish, Norwegian "Landsmaal," and Faroese.

Of MacDiarmid's discovery of the imaginative potentialities of Scots—"an experience akin to that of religious conversion"[25]—much will be said later in discussing his poetry. What needs to be made clear at this point is that, on hearing of the efforts of the Vernacular Circle in

London, he suddenly realised that he had been educated in Scotland (a country once famous for its educational system) without learning anything worth knowing about its native literature, much less actually reading it. He knew a few poems by Burns, and as a Border man of course he knew a number of traditional ballads, but that was all. Of Henryson, Dunbar, and Douglas, who wrote in the later fifteenth and early sixteenth centuries when Scots was as potent a literary language as any in Europe, he knew precisely nothing. He was equally ignorant of the factors that caused the decline of that language into local dialects—*e.g.*, the adoption in Reformation Scotland of an *English* translation of the Bible—and was barely even aware of the eighteenth-century vernacular revival of which Burns was the culmination.

Such ignorance was nothing unusual amongst Scotsmen, and as he became conscious of the extent to which his nation had lost its own traditions in the process of Anglicisation, he took it upon himself to "keep up perpetually a sort of Berserker rage" of protest, and to act as "the catfish that vitalizes the other torpid denizens of the aquarium."[26] He set about acquiring an enormous knowledge of all matters concerning Scotland, and to every pro-English tendency he opposed an anti-English one—and then some more. After all, he had recently returned from a war fought for the rights of small nations, and "Scotland is the oldest independent monarchy in Europe. It is the only white man's country—with the exception of Wales—that hasn't got a measure of Home Rule."[27] Or so he says.

MacDiarmid's political nationalism grew out of his reading of Scottish history and literature, but it was certainly affected by contemporary developments in Ireland, and the extremity of his views should be placed in relation to the social and economic conditions of the time. The clearest picture of all this is to be found in his *Albyn* (1927), which should be read along with George

Malcolm Thomson's *Caledonia* (to which it is, in part, an answer) and the same author's *Scotland: That Distressed Area* (1934).

The baiting of Anglo-Scots and English apart, MacDiarmid's nationalism is not at all narrow but is rather conceived as the necessary condition of internationalism. For him, it is the veneered cosmopolite who lacks understanding of the differing points of view of different peoples, because he does not proceed from an adequate understanding of his own people. On the other hand, one of MacDiarmid's principal reasons for urging complete independence from England is that he believes the English to be inveterately insular while the Scots are (or were, and will be again) international-minded.

Even linguistically, MacDiarmid's greatest hope for Scotland lay, not in the vernacular Braid Scots—a northern development of what in the south has become "standard" English—but in Gaelic. In his pamphlet, *Scotland in 1980*, he envisaged the re-establishment of the ancient Gaelic Commonwealth in Scotland, with "80 per cent of all the creative literature of any value" being written in Gaelic.[28]

His conception of the "Gaelic Idea" was, from the first, international—a sort of Pan-Celtism that would counterpoise an ancient culture, at once aristocratic and popular, against the dictatorship of the proletariat as that was manifesting itself in Russia. It might be as far-fetched as Dostoevsky's "Russian Idea," but he conceived it to be, like the latter, a "dynamic myth"[29]—and at least it suggested a nobler prospect for Scotland's future than was offered by the Decline and Fall of the British Empire. In MacDiarmid's later conception, the need to "polarize Russia effectively" is replaced with the discovery of a common cause by the Slav and the Celt, in both of whom East and West are said to meet; and he sees it as his personal task to "work for the establishment of Workers' Republics in Scotland, Ireland, Wales and Cornwall,

and, indeed, make a sort of Celtic Union of Socialist
Soviet Republics in the British Isles."[30]

In the words of Edwin Muir, MacDiarmid is "everything that is out and out."[31] A life-long extremist on
principle, he "despises scruples," as his most loyal friend
has said,[32] and yet he cannot resist any opportunity for
self-justification. In the "Prelude" to *Scottish Scene* (1934),
a book in which he collaborated with "Lewis Grassic
Gibbon" (James Leslie Mitchell—another of the curious
tribe of pseudonymous Scots), he wrote that

> He sees his land as a unity too,
> And creation in terms of it.
>
> The future concerns him even more
> Than the past or the present do;
> He boasts of his proleptic power
> —And is entitled to![33]

Typically, the truth that is here expressed is obscured by
the truculent tone, which is an habitual part of his role
as an intellectual tough. That truth is concerned, not as it
might seem with simple futurity, but rather with *possibility*, which is of course referable to past, present, and
future. And the unity he lays claim to is imaginative, not
logical:

> I am a poet; our fools ask me for logic not life![34]

He has always been "immensely more interested in the
vaguest adumbration of what we might have been than
in any possible development of what we are."[35] His
premises are not amongst those to which we have become
comfortably accustomed. The free play of conflicting and
contradictory ideas is for him the most vital intellectual
exercise whereby consciousness is extended; and his work
from first to last may best be understood in the light of a
statement he made in 1926: "The function of art is the
extension of human consciousness."[36]

REFERENCES

1. Quoted in *L.P.*, p. 411.
2. From Marcus Aurelius. See *L.P.*, p. 423.
3. A pamphlet of which 50 copies were privately printed by Joseph W. Sault, n.p. or d.
4. Sydney Goodsir Smith, in a radio programme, "The Indivisible Man," by Norman McCaig, B.B.C. Scottish Home Service, 3 Jul. 1957.
5. *L.P.*, p. 226.
6. *L.P.*, p. 231.
7. *L.P.*, pp. 8–9.
8. *L.P.*, p. 232.
9. *L.P.*, p. 227.
10. *L.P.*, p. 328.
11. *L.P.*, p. vii.
12. Henry D. Harben, *The Rural Problem*, London 1913. See "Preface," p. vi.
13. "Aims and Opinions," 2nd of two recorded conversations with D. G. Bridson, B.B.C. Third Programme, 9 Mar. 1960.
14. *N.R.*, Sep. 1924, pp. 297–9.
15. *L.P.*, pp. 143–5.
16. *L.P.*, pp. 41, 44.
17. See letter in *Scotsman*, 5 Dec. 1932.
18. "Talking with Five Thousand People in Edinburgh," in *Poetry—Scotland*, 2nd Collection, p. 50.
19. "Aims and Opinions," 9 Mar. 1960.
20. *L.P.*, p. 67.
21. "MacDiarmid—The Man," in *Jabberwock* (Edinburgh University Review), VOL. V, 1958, pp. 14–16.
22. *L.P.*, p. 149.
23. Open letter by Lewis Spence, quoted in *C.S.S.*, p. 14.
24. *B.C.*, 1923, pp. 26–38. Reprinted in *The Scottish Tongue*, London 1924.
25. Radio talk, "The Use of Scots and English," B.B.C. Scottish Home Service, 18 Dec. 1956.
26. *L.P.*, pp. 79, xv.
27. "Aims and Opinions," 9 Mar. 1960.
28. *Op. cit.*, p. 4.
29. "The Caledonian Antisyzygy and the Gaelic Idea," *M.S.*, Jul. 1931, pp. 141–54; and Jan. 1932, pp. 333–7.
30. *L.P.*, p. 26.
31. From a letter quoted in P. H. Butter, *Edwin Muir*, Edinburgh, 1962, p. 29.
32. Norman McCaig, in "The Indivisible Man."
33. *S.Sc.*, p. 15.
34. *S.L.*, p. 53.
35. "The Assault on Humanism," in *S.N.*, 16 Oct. 1923, p. 4.
36. "Art and the Unknown," in *N.A.*, 20 May 1926, p. 23.

CHAPTER II

EARLY VERSE AND PROSE

The early verse is by Grieve, not MacDiarmid, and it is in English. Sequences of fifty and a hundred sonnets are referred to in various places, but not many of the poems have appeared in print. The principal sources are: the three volumes of *Northern Numbers* (1920-1-2), an experiment in group publication which aimed at doing for contemporary poetry in Scotland what the *Georgian Poetry* series had done in England; some issues of Grieve's literary monthly, *Scottish Chapbook* (1922-3); and Grieve's first book, *Annals of the Five Senses* (1923), in which poems alternate with prose pieces.

The three issues of *Northern Numbers*, edited by Grieve, show a characteristic ruthlessness in using and later discarding established names (John Buchan, Neil Munro) and even titles (General Sir Ian Hamilton, the Rev. Lauchlan MacLean Watt, D.D.). Only John Fergusson shared with the editor himself the distinction of appearing in all three volumes. True, there is better poetry in the last issue than in the other two; there is also a curious increase in the number of female contributors—from about 10 to 30 to 50 per cent.

Taken all together, Grieve's poems are not markedly better than some of the others—they are too uneven for that—but they are certainly more interesting. It is a mistake to suppose, as some commentators have done, that because his group-publishing venture was an imitation of *Georgian Poetry*, Grieve's poems were imitations of the Georgian style of writing—whatever that is taken to be. There is a sense in which the admirable "Cattle

Show" (reprinted in *Stony Limits*) may be called Georgian, but it is not imitative of anything in particular; and although the poem "Heaven" takes its starting point from Rupert Brooke, it ends up in different territory.

"Georgian" is in any case an irritatingly vague term, but its particular irrelevance with regard to Grieve's early work will be clear enough if one tries to imagine the erotic-religious imagery of his "Water of Life" in the context of Edward Marsh's collections. Or consider these lines from "The Wind-Bags":

> Rain-beaten stones: great tussocks of dead grass
> And stagnant waters throwing leaden lights
> To leaden skys: a rough-maned wind that bites
> With aimless violence at the clouds that pass,
> Roaring, blackjowled, and bull-like in the void,
> And I, in wild and boundless consciousness,
> A brooding chaos, feel within me press
> The corpse of Time, aborted, cold, negroid.[1]

That "negroid" foetus could never have got into a Georgian woodpile, unless D. H. Lawrence had smuggled it in. And the strongly erotic element in several of the other poems—"Consummation" (a description of the sexual act), "Spanish Girl," "The Following Day," for example—is something very much closer to the Belgian Albert Giraud than to any of the English group. Giraud is mentioned specifically because a phrase from a poem of his, translated as "Youth Among the Lilies" by Jethro Bithell,[2] is echoed in Grieve's "Water of Life."[3] Grieve had a very extensive knowledge of contemporary European poetry, at any rate in translation, as may be seen from numerous articles contributed by him to *The New Age* between April 1924 and September 1928. So far as work in translation is concerned, he was clearly a leading authority on the subject.

Two main points may be made about the early verse in English. Firstly, Grieve shows that hypersensitivity to words which is the fundamental sign of talent in a young poet—his poem "The Last Chord" was obviously contrived in order to use the phrase "That carefully-shaded sevenfold Amen"[4]—but his over-all sense of style is so shaky that he sometimes lapses into bathos and sometimes is carried along merely by the momentum of the words themselves. Secondly, he shows in several of these poems a sort of cosmogonical eye—presenting a God's-eye-view of the created universe—that was to become deeply characteristic of his work. This may be seen in "Acme," "Within That Week," "Mountain Measure," "Playmates," "The Last Song," and "Science and Poetry":

> All-conscious Earth serenely swinging
> In its appointed place
> Is flawed by no least trace
> Of chaos to it clinging;
> And all that all men are and have
> Is one green-gleaming point of light
> In infinite night.[5]

Of his aggressive nationalism there is little sign, though he becomes as nostalgic at times as any other soldier in exile, and a note informs us that his five "Sonnets of the Highland Hills" were part of a privately-circulated sequence of fifty on that theme. As a matter of fact, the title of Grieve's book, *Annals of the Five Senses*, is a phrase used by Gregory Smith with reference to the national characteristics of the Scottish Muse.[6] But young poets do not necessarily distinguish very clearly between their Muse and the person they are in love with at the time. Hence one should be wary of reading too much into the statement of Grieve, the "Scots Borderman" in the poem "Allegiance," that

> my heart is hers whose shy, light eyes
> And small, swift smile elate

Sealed me the servant of a cause forlorn,
  Whose dream and whose desire I cannot tell,
Where timeless silence in the far blue hills
  Hangs like a ready bell.[7]

"Characteristically, thoughts of women led to thoughts
religious," says the author of the *Annals*;[8] and the most
impressive poem in that book is the only early poem of a
religious nature that is free from frankly erotic imagery.
However, the feminine principle is not absent but is
rather concealed in the poem in question, "A Moment in
Eternity,"[9] which suggests, through a symbolic imagery
of leaves, light, wind, and flame, a mystical intuition of
union with the divine creative power. Denis Saurat wrote
an interpretation of this poem in terms of his own
"Actuel" philosophy,[10] but it is more useful to know
something of the philosophy of Soloviev, and in particular his conception of Hagia Sophia, which influenced
Russian symbolist poets such as Alexander Blok, in
whom Grieve was specially interested.[11] Given the
belief in a personal, masculine God, Soloviev believed
that the cosmos also has a personality, which is feminine.
This is Sophia, the Wisdom of God, and she figures in
Grieve's poem as the "new light," the "new tree," that
stands unmoved in the heart of God while all other
personalities change endlessly with His dreams, an
"essential element and conscious part" of which they are:

  —A white light like a silence
  Accentuating the great songs!
  —A shining silence wherein God
  Might see as in a mirror
  The miracles that He must next achieve. . . .

  O Thou,
  Who art the wisdom of the God
  Whose ecstasies we are!

"A Moment in Eternity" belongs to the European symbolist movement in poetry, and its roots go back through Russia to France. It is notable for its carefully contrived sound-patterns, and it is sharply distinguished from mystical poetry of the more hazy, emotional variety by a sort of incandescence of *mind* at the centre of it:

> —Meteors for roots,
> And my topmost spires
> Notes of enchanted light
> Blind in the Godhead!
> —White stars at noon!
>
> I shone within my thoughts
> As God within us shines.

Of the six prose pieces in the *Annals*, the most successful are the least ambitious: "Café-Scene" and "Sartoria." The first of these may be associated with the fact that Grieve had been invalided home from the army with cerebral malaria; at all events, it depicts a physical and mental condition similar to that caused by a fever, and does so brilliantly. The other is a sort of mosaic built up from items about dress, especially female dress, which suggests that fashion magazines must have been included in the author's voracious reading. It also reveals the passion for specialised terms and esoteric vocabularies that has characterised so much of his later work: "I left him at the Haymarket standing in the centre of the pavement murmuring over and over again, 'Nainsook Directoire knickers trimmed with Swiss insertion'."[12]

A third piece, "The Never-Yet-Explored," would be included among the really successful ones but for the clumsy way in which the author's reading is foisted on to a character who is intended to be the centre of attention in her own right. This is indicative of a fault that also spoils "Cerebral." Although the author's relationship to his subject-matter is often extremely subtle, his relationship with the reader can be startlingly naïve. The reason for this may be found in Grieve's "obscure but poignant sense of being an entirely different person to himself."[13] He is liable to stop his narrative and point to this "entirely different person," asking the reader if he ever saw anything remotely approaching *that* before, and forgetting that from the reader's angle he is simply pointing to himself. Whatever else may be said about this curious phenomenon, which is recurrent in his work, it has too often had the effect of throwing the work out of perspective and irritating or indeed antagonising the reader.

It is difficult to classify these prose pieces or briefly to describe them. Grieve himself refers to them as "these psychological studies, essays, mosaics (call them what you will) which I have (perhaps the best word in the meantime is) 'designed'."[14] Presumably he prefers the term "designed" to "written" because he is often working mosaic-fashion with material quarried from the huge mass of reading stored away in his head or in his notebooks. In the longest of these works, "A Four Years' Harvest," the method is at its weakest and we are left looking back towards the quarries from which the various items came instead of focusing on the design which they are intended to make.

Edwin Muir said when the *Annals* first appeared that the style struck him as being "in almost every way original and unusual":[15] but part of the impression of originality comes from the fact that Grieve is immensely more eclectic than anyone else. One cannot derive his style from particular sources because the sources are so many and so fantastically varied. This has obvious dangers, and Grieve speaks of his fear of having "paralysed his creative faculties by over-reading." What saved him from this in the end was the intense activity of a "tiny specialist cell in his brain" which constantly experimented with an "obscure ray . . . emanating from his subtle realisation that beyond the individual mind of each man was a collective mind"—that is, the "collective unconscious" of

Jung. "The little specialist was able to use this pretty much as a man uses electricity or radium. The consequence was that he was enabled . . . to trace the thin line of his own mentality through all the incalculable fabric of the thought of humanity. This gave him latitude and longitude on the oceans of speculation."[16] Sometimes! Often enough, at any rate, to give Muir "that impression which can only be produced by the entry of a new personality, a new potentiality, into literature."

Grieve at this time was evidently immersed in psychology, but it was the psychology of *intellectual* processes that mainly held his interest. He is like a man who carries around with him a fascinating specimen—his own brain, preserved in "a strong solution of books" and constantly subjected to shock treatment by the mass media of the modern world, especially magazines and newspapers. He pays minute attention to the effects of this bombardment of the brain, reverberating within an almost limitless memory, and gives the reader a running commentary on his observations. When the bombardment is most violent, so is the style of the observer, who keeps throwing parenthesis after parenthesis into false-bottomed sentences. Of course the brain is also subjected to sense impressions, and these are reported as well, but the observer is most interested in particles of intellectual information, ideas, facts.

At the end of it all the reader, a little exhausted, may feel that he has been left with some extraordinarily interesting fragments, but to fit them into a total design is quite another matter. Yet, on reflexion, one can see certain basic patterns emerging from the *chaos décoratif*. One of these may be picked out by way of example:

He could not help wondering . . . whether intelligence itself was not an accident in the creative processes, or really the goal towards which mankind believed itself drifting. . . . He fell back on the old, old feeling that . . . if every opinion is equally insignificant in itself, humanity's bewilderment of thought is a mighty net which somehow holds the whole truth. . . .

So his tendency was always to the whole, to the totality, to the general balance of things. Indeed it was his chiefest difficulty (and an ever-increasing one that made him fear at times cancellation to nonentity) to exclude, to condemn, to say No. Here, probably, was the secret of the way in which he used to plunge into the full current of the most inconsistent movements, seeking, always in vain, until he was utterly exhausted . . . to find ground upon which he might stand foursquare. . . .

He was always fighting for the absent, eager for forlorn hopes, a champion of the defeated cause, for those portions of truth which seemed to him neglected. . . .[17]

REFERENCES

1. *N.N.*, 2nd Series, p. 54.
2. *Contemporary Belgian Poetry*, London 1911, p. 59.
3. *N.N.*, 3rd Series, p. 56.
4. *N.N.*, 3rd Series, p. 59.
5. *S.C.*, Nov. 1922, p. 105.
6. *Scottish Literature*, London 1919, p. 33.
7. *N.N.*, 1st Series, p. 68.
8. *A.*, p. 79.
9. *A.*, pp. 27–33 (1–6).
10. *S.N.*, 3 Jul. 1923, p. 5.
11. Vladimir Soloviev, *La Russie et L'Eglise universelle*, Paris 1889.
12. *A.*, p. 139.
13. *A.*, p. 13.
14. *A.*, Dedication to John Buchan.
15. "Readers and Writers," *N.A.*, 15 Nov. 1923, pp. 32–3.
16. *A.*, p. 19.
17. *A.*, pp. 15, 194–5.

CHAPTER III

PARNASSUS AND SCHIEHALLION[1]

Wha ^abourds wi' thee had need be wary,   ^a provokes,
And ^blear wi' skill thy thrust to parry,   mocks at.
When thou consults thy dictionary   ^b learn.
    Of ancient words,
Which come from thy poetic quarry
    As sharp as swords.

WM. HAMILTON to ALLAN RAMSAY, 1719.

In May 1922 letters from Grieve began to appear in various newspapers, canvassing for subscribers to a new monthly chapbook of current Scottish poetry. The first number of this periodical, *The Scottish Chapbook*, appeared in August of that year, and it was clear from the beginning that Grieve had in mind something much bigger than the *Northern Numbers* idea. In his first editorial, he recalled a short-lived "Scots Renascence" movement which had centred around Patrick Geddes in Edinburgh and issued four numbers of a lavish periodical called *The Evergreen* between spring 1895 and winter 1896–7. This had disappeared into the Celtic Twilight, and "the movement of which it was the organ scarcely outlasted it. . . . The Scottish literary revival proved to be a promise that could not be kept."[2] Obviously, Grieve intended to make, and keep, a greater promise, and when Denis Saurat used the term "renaissance écossaise" about the *Scottish Chapbook* group he was only echoing Grieve himself, who had avowed his belief in the possibility of "a great Scottish Literary Renaissance" in February 1923.[3] However, "Renaissance" is one of the big words that make us so unhappy, as Joyce put it, and the infant mortality rate of the new movement was high.

Grieve did his best to swell the ranks by becoming two people, as William Sharp ("Fiona Macleod") had done before him, in the new *Evergreen* and elsewhere, and indeed as an extraordinary number of Scottish writers have done in recent times. "Hugh MacDiarmid" made his *début* in the first number of the *Scottish Chapbook*, and since Grieve has adopted this name almost to the exclusion of his patronymic, we shall follow his usage from now onwards.

MacDiarmid's first work was not a poem in Scots, as is often supposed, but a sketchily-dramatised piece of English prose called "Nisbet: An Interlude in Post-War Glasgow." It is of no great literary value, but the hero, Nisbet, has much in common with the author himself[4] and casts a good deal of light on a matter of some importance: MacDiarmid's conception of Russia's role in history. Tacitly paraphrasing Spengler to the effect that all forms of literary and intellectual expression had reached a dead-end in Western Europe and America, Nisbet declares that "we must wait . . . for the new beginning which will come from a civilization other than ours." And Young, the Communist propagandist who plays Judas to Nisbet's Christ, tells him that "the renewal is coming, has begun to come, from Russia. . . . In Dostoevsky is to be found the first delineation of that new world."[5] Judas or not, it is with Young that Nisbet goes off at the end of the sketch.

This theme was not developed, at least in MacDiarmid's poetry, until *A Drunk Man Looks At The Thistle* appeared in 1926. In the meanwhile, an event of very great importance in Scottish literary history took place.

MacDiarmid has confessed to having known very little about Scots literature when he opposed the foundation in 1920 of the Vernacular Circle of the London Burns Club. By August 1922, however, active support of "the campaign of the Vernacular Circle . . . for the revival of the Doric" was included in the programme for his *Chapbook*—a programme which insisted on a "distinctly

Scottish range of values" and aimed to "encourage and publish the work of contemporary Scottish poets and dramatists, whether in English, Gaelic, or Braid Scots." In the September issue of the magazine, Rebecca West's novel about Edinburgh, *The Judge*, was reviewed by someone called Martin Gillespie (*another* pseudonym?), and the following month there appeared a "Monologue in the Vernacular" entitled "Following Rebecca West in Edinburgh" by Hugh MacDiarmid. There are actually two voices in this "monologue," one of which comments admiringly in English on the use of Scots by the other. The theme is the need for a Scottish James Joyce who would do for Edinburgh what *Ulysses* had just done (in February of that year) for Dublin, and it is postulated that such a writer would find in the old Scots vernacular the verbal compost needed for his purposes.[7]

What follows is a phenomenon familiar to readers of MacDiarmid's later poetry: the subject of his writing is the kind of writing he would like to be able to write and hopes will eventually be written. It seems to have originated in a habit MacDiarmid acquired in the course of his early training in journalism, a profession in which developments are sometimes reported before they have actually occurred. Not that it is only journalists who substitute the advance hand-out for the reality, but it is MacDiarmid the literary journalist, I think, who offers us the advance hand-out as a form of literature.

"Following Rebecca West in Glasgow" might be called a hoax, but it is more the work of a journalist in a hurry than of a deliberate hoaxer. One need not go further than the first three letters of the alphabet in Jamieson's *Etymological Dictionary of the Scottish Language* to find the more unfamiliar part of the Scots vocabulary used by MacDiarmid, and most of his quotations and references to literary works in Scots are there as well. Hoaxers are more careful about covering their tracks.

Nor is this simply a literary joke. MacDiarmid's sense

of humour is sufficiently daft for any enormity, but there
is here also a kind of "literal-mindedness" that is of serious
value to a poet, especially when combined with a touch
of that "mania" which Coleridge saw as an analogue for
certain aspects of the creative imagination.

The extraordinary fact is that in the middle of this
lexicographical junkyard MacDiarmid found "the stone
that the builders rejected" and fashioned the first of a
number of lyrics that are amongst the finest of modern
times. His first poem in Scots, "The Watergaw," appeared in this same number of the *Scottish Chapbook*, and
its distinctive quality was immediately recognised. It is
not one of his most typical, nor perhaps one of his very
best lyrics, but it should be quoted here both for its
historical priority and for the evidence it presents of
MacDiarmid's sureness of touch and feeling for rhythm
when handling his new medium for the first time in verse:

> Ae weet forenicht i' the yow-trummle
> I saw yon antrin thing,
> A watergaw wi' its chitterin' licht
> Ayont the on-ding;
> An' I thocht o' the last wild look ye gied
> Afore ye deed!
>
> There was nae reek i' the laverock's hoose
> That nicht—an' nane i' mine;
> But I hae thocht o' that foolish licht
> Ever sin' syne;
> An' I think that mebbe at last I ken
> What your look meant then.[8]

The author, in the person of C. M. Grieve, the editor
of *Scottish Chapbook*, was able immediately to comment on
his own work as follows:

Doric economy of expressiveness is impressively illustrated in the first four lines of Mr. MacDiarmid's
poem. Translate them into English. That is the test.

You will find that the shortest possible translation runs something like this: "One wet afternoon (or early evening) in the cold weather in July after the sheep-shearing I saw that rare thing—an indistinct rainbow, with its shivering light, above the heavily-falling rain."[9]

Now, although one may object to the loose rendering of "ayont" [beyond] as "above," and the unidiomatic use of "antrin," there is no doubt about the expressive economy of such a word as "yow-trummle." "Yow-trummle" (literally "ewe-tremble," because the sheep have been shorn before this late cold-spell arrives) is a kind of ready-made metaphor, as is the strange idiom of "There was nae reek [smoke] i' the laverock's hoose [lark's house]," which MacDiarmid glosses as meaning "It was a dark and stormy night."

In availing himself of such rich and concentrated resources of language, the poet was not concerned with whether any particular expression became officially obsolete ages ago, or was used only within a twelve-mile radius of Kirkcudbright in 1899. But, on the other hand, neither was he systematically building up what Saurat termed a "synthetic" language with the help of Jamieson and the "Golconda of racy old terms" he found in George Beattie's *John o' Arnha'* and William Nicholson's *Brownie of Blednock*. Rather, he approached Scots words, *any* Scots words, as potential material for poetry, and relied on his sensitivity towards verbal stimuli to select what his imagination could put to use in a poem.

The fact that there were plenty of precedents for writing in an amalgam of "synthetic" Scots, drawn from different dialects and different historical periods, is interesting: but there is no need to cite it as a justification of MacDiarmid's practice. One does not have to know that, for example, Robert Burns to some extent employed such an amalgam in order to appreciate the excellence of a poem by MacDiarmid.

C

But Burns is popularly regarded as a model of natural-ness—at the farthest remove from the sort of poet who would ransack dictionaries for words and phrases to be used as a framework on which to build poems, as MacDiarmid sometimes does. A great deal depends on our conception of what is "natural" and what "artificial" in verbal creative activity. MacDiarmid took his stand with Mallarmé, "the act of poetry being the reverse of what it is normally thought to be; not an idea gradually shaping itself in words, but deriving entirely from words." It was in this way, he says, that he wrote all the best of his Scots poems.[10]

The fact that a word is unfamiliar, obsolescent, or obsolete is not in itself a disadvantage and may in fact prove an advantage to a poet, as "The Watergaw" will show. One can see, clearly enough, how difficult it would be in English to juxtapose a symbolic rainbow and the last look of a dying person (the poet's father in this case) without leaving an impression of sentimentality or at any rate of emotional blatancy. This is largely because "rainbow" has built-in literary connotations. For the reader of poetry, it is hard to free it from the accretions of the several generations of romanticism since Wordsworth. But if "watergaw" is known to the reader at all it has no ready-made associations other than those attaching to a countryman's observation of the weather—hardly a sentimental activity—and it does not even denote a "rainbow" but rather a fragmentary or indistinct kind of rainbow—a precise word for a hazy phenomenon. Simi-larly, "yow-trummle" is fresh and appealing because the word is still clean. The pathetically fallacious poetasters and vendors of whimsicality who so abounded in Scot-land after Burns did not have the chance of sugar-coating it, since it remained hidden between the covers of Jamieson. Hence, as MacDiarmid pointed out when the poem made its initial appearance, the language of "The Watergaw" is "disfigured by none of the usual senti-mentality" found in Scots verse at least since Burns's time.

That is not to say that sentimentality cannot be read into the poem, as in fact more than one commentary on it has shown. "The Watergaw" depends for its effect on leaving the reader guessing as he finishes it, and he will not see the clue offered him with deliberate ambiguity in the word "foolish" (in the ninth line) if his mind's eye is blinded with a too-ready tear. Indeed, this is an excellent example of the kind of poem that people can feel they know and enjoy and appreciate without ever having really read it—a fact that does much to account for its general popularity.

More typically, the imagery of MacDiarmid's early Scots lyrics is "realised" within the poems themselves. In quite a number of these, the cosmogonical eye already noted is brought into sharper focus through his use of Scots words—words which most commonly identify natural phenomena in a country setting—and the result of this, together with a compressed, sometimes laconic or sarcastic turn of phrase, is MacDiarmid's own brand of imagism. Only one of the English poems he was writing at this time combines an imagist slant with the appropriate terseness—an epigram which appeared in the *Scottish Chapbook* for December 1922. It is interesting to compare this with a Scots poem, "The Eemis Stane," which is very close to it in date:

Four wreathes a year old Time brings still
—No other mourner visiteth
This lonely stone of Earth that marks
The resting place of Life and Death.[11]

The Eemis Stane

I' the how-dumb-deid o' the cauld hairst nicht
The warl' like an eemis stane
Wags i' the lift;
An' my eerie memories fa'
Like a yowdendrift.

Like a yowdendrift so's I couldna read
The words cut oot i' the stane
Had the fug o' fame
An' history's hazelraw
No' yirdit thaim.* [12]

A certain amount of patience is required of readers
unfamiliar with the Scots vocabulary, of course, but its
difficulty is often much less than might appear at first
glance. For example, the component parts of the word
"how-dumb-deid" are quite ordinary words, though it
would be easier to recognise the first one if it were
spelled "howe" (a hollow). We have a habit of reacting
to unfamiliar words as though their unfamiliarity to us
implied artificiality in their use by the writer: but the fact
is that MacDiarmid's *use* of the word "visiteth" in his
English poem is more truly artificial than his *use* of
"how-dumb-deid" or "yowdendrift." And the more
closely one scrutinises "The Eemis Stane" the more one
gets from it. It will stand up to repeated readings long
after the initial strangeness of the words has disappeared.
On the other hand, if one looks closely at the English
poem one begins to see through it. It seems to be part
soul, part skeleton, as MacDiarmid once said of a
thwarted thistle. The abstract (Time, Life, Death) and
the concrete (the stone) are articulated only by a
rhetorical machinery of personification, and the movement becomes increasingly mechanical. But the Scots
poem has body, and its rhythm has at once more subtlety
and more of the conviction of living emotion. And this
despite the fact that some of the Scots words have been
issued with death certificates by the lexicographers.

One notices also that the imagery of "The Eemis

* In the still centre of the dead of night, cold at harvest time, the
world like a teetering stone sways in the sky; and my eerie memories
fall like snow driven by the wind. Like snow driven by the wind, so
that I couldn't read the words cut out on the stone, even if the moss of
fame and the lichens of history had not buried them.

Stane" can be fully visualised in a way in which that of the English poem can not, at least without ensuing embarrassment. One averts one's eyes from the spectacle of Old Father Time, punctilious wreath in hand, looking around for support—as well he might, in view of the fact that the seasons are continuing to change although life and death have ceased. There is, too, an element of unconscious censorship in the choice of the euphemistic expression "resting place" from which MacDiarmid was released when he wrote in Scots.

Even the difficulty caused by unfamiliar words is not necessarily a bad thing for the reader of poetry. By their very unfamiliarity, they sharpen our perceptions of verbal qualities to which we habitually pay too little attention, and invite a more positive response from our imaginations. With our faculties thus tuned up, we expect a lot more from our author than just Rossetti's "stunning words for poetry." And we get it.

"The Eemis Stane" has style, in a distinctive sense in which the author of the early poems in English lacked style. This is one of the many things that cannot be learned from a dictionary. And as one reads the best of the Scots lyrics one realises that the style has been hall-marked by MacDiarmid. One has the sensation of a great talent finding itself in a medium, as he himself put it, "to which up to then I had never given a thought."[13]

A number of these poems have a characteristic kind of imagery which comes from the combination of an eye for the cosmic with the countrified, blunt-spoken quality, of the earth earthy, that is associated with colloquial Scots. Or perhaps, remembering what MacDiarmid has said about the essentially verbal nature of poetic composition, the words should come first in the combination. The two elements seem not unlike the chicken and the egg, however. Consider the following passage of Scots prose, in which he begins by recalling the names of the various marbles he used to play with as a boy, and goes on to say

that it is particularly when he becomes aware of the
cosmos that the words are conjured up again:

> Glessies as bricht as Jenny's een, wi' coloured twirls
> inside them, and white cheeny anes, and green anes oot
> o' the taps o' lemonade bottles. Clay-davies, doolies,
> hard-hacks, mavies, cracksie-pigs, cullies—I'd a' the
> kinds. I mind o' them every time I see the stars reelin',
> and I can hardly look at a picter o' the globe—aye, or at
> the earth itsel' for the maitter o' that, as you whiles see
> it, no' in a toon, whaur it's a' crancrums and stour, but
> frae a braw brae tap, when you seem to see the haill o't
> birlin' clear as a penny afore you—withoot wantin'
> to cry 'Holie for Nags!'[14]

From this point of view, the fantastic, sometimes
grotesque ingredient in MacDiarmid's imagery, and
especially in his cosmic high jinks, may be seen as the
most natural of things, for its associations are with childhood, with the marvels of "bairn sang"—where the cow
jumps over the moon just like that—and the imaginative
lore of the folk. There certainly seems to be a connexion
between the quoted passage about boyhood games and
the fantastic cosmic imagery—which is nonetheless clear,
hard, and objectively, often dramatically, presented—of
such poems as the "suite" called "Au Clair de la Lune,"
in which the earth is a spinning top or a stone, while the
moon is a disreputable "craw [crow] o' a body" sitting
on the four cross-winds, or a piper, or a huntress with the
oceans for her dogs. The same is true of "Morning," in
which the sun is plunked in the sky like a frog in a cream-
basin; "Krang," where the earth is the hulk of a whale
whose bleached bones are taken by the wind for a harp;
and "Somersault," in which West and East on the spinning world become "the pigs at Gadara" and "a sow at
the farrow." These cosmic conceits, if that is the word for
them, seem to have been suggested to MacDiarmid's
imagination by an interaction between vernacular words

and boyhood memories, and they have a primitive
quality that might link them with the "collective unconscious of the race," as his early interest in Jung may well
have suggested to him. But if there are archetypal
images in these poems, they come from his imaginative
exploration of the language rather than from textbooks
of psychology.

It is this primitive appeal that makes it seem so
natural that MacDiarmid should have a view of the
cosmos in

> the light that breaks
> From the whole earth seen as a star again
> In the general life of man.[15]

And, in turn, it was a tremendous gain for him to be able
to express such a view in words that were clean and fresh
and hard in outline, rather than smeared and bleared
and smudged. As used by him, a large part of the Scots
vocables had that advantage, and along with it the
raucle-tongued, earthy quality already mentioned, that
ensured that the cosmic view would not dissolve into the
airy-fairy. When the words are of the kind associated in
his mind with childhood, we get, not sentimentality, but
sheer devilment:

> Men see their warld turned *a*tapsalteerie,
> *b*Drookit in a licht *c*owre eerie,
> Or sent *d*birlin' like a *e*peerie—
> Syne it turns a' they've kent till then
> To shapes they can nae langer ken.[16]

a head-over-heels
b drowned
c too
d spinning
e top

All this may seem a far cry from T. E. Hulme and the
Imagists, who no doubt were conjured up by the previous
reference to MacDiarmid's brand of imagism. In his
prose writings about this time MacDiarmid shows that he
was familiar with Hulme's ideas, and in one of his Scots
poems, "God Takes a Rest,"[17] he makes use of an image

that Hulme seems to have stolen from Victor Hugo's "Mendiant" for his poem "The Embankment." There is no question of MacDiarmid merely imitating Hulme or other Imagists, but a number of his Scots poems present single images or make use of visual juxtapositions, and they could be used to illustrate the imagist principles of having an "actually realised visual object" in mind, of observing a drastic economy in the use of words, and of concentrating upon hard, clear, dry qualities in order to avoid "emotional slither." For example, "Overinzievar":

The pigs shoot up their [a]gruntles here,   [a] snouts
The hens staund [b]hullerie,   [b] with ruffled
And a' the [c]hinds glower roond about   feathers
Wi' unco dullery.   [c] farmservants

Wi' [a]sook-the-bluids and [b]switchables   [a] little red beetles
The grund's fair [c]crottled up,   [b] earwigs
And [d]owre't the forkit lichtnin' flees   [c] crumbled
Like a [e]cleisher o' a [f]whup.[18]   [d] over it
    [e] lash   [f] whip

On the other hand, the imagist group's preoccupation with *vers libre* cadences did not concern MacDiarmid, because he found that in Scots he could achieve fresh and interesting rhythmical effects within the old lyric framework of metre and rhyme. This was to some extent "maken vertu of necessittee," since the traditional short lyric is the only unbroken tradition in Scots verse, and where rhythm was concerned MacDiarmid was bound to train his ear on this, on folk-song and ballad, and on speech rhythm, any other kind of living continuity being non-existent. "Empty Vessel" will show what he achieved:

I met [a]ayont the [b]cairney   [a] beyond   [b] little cairn
A lass wi' tousie hair
Singin' till a bairnie
That was nae langer there.

^aWunds wi' warlds to swing   ^a winds
^bDinna sing sae sweet,   ^b don't
The licht that bends ^cowre ^da'thing ^c over   ^d everything
Is less ta'en up wi't.[19]

In these eight lines MacDiarmid may be seen to be
instinctively tapping elements in the old ballads that
were particularly sympathetic to the bent of his own
mind: the stark treatment of mystery or tragedy, the
details of which are left to the imagination; the switch
without transition from the natural to the more-than-
natural; and the defiant acceptance of suffering as the
distinction as well as the inevitable condition of human
life. As to rhythm, he took a suggestion from a rough old
folk-song and transformed it mightily. The song has only
recently been identified as the anonymous "Jennie
Nettles" by George Bruce,[20] who found it in Herd's
Ancient and Modern Scots Songs (first published in 1769).
The relevant verse runs as follows:

I met ayont the Kairney,
    Jenny Nettles, Jenny Nettles,
Singing till her bairny,
    Robin Rattle's bastard;
To flee the ^adool upo' the ^bstool,   ^a sorrow   ^b (of repent-
    And ^cilka ane that mocks her,   ance)
She round about seeks Robin out,   ^c every one
    To stap it in his ^doxter.[21]   ^d armpit

MacDiarmid used such material as this with an instinct
for rhythm so convincing that it can make even so conventional a line as "Dinna sing sae sweet" seem "right"
with the rightness of the inevitable. Notice how the turn
from countrified to cosmic imagery in his second stanza
is accompanied by a change in rhythm, supported by
alliteration and internal rhyme. This is beautifully judged
art, but the supreme touch comes at the end with the
off-beat (both rhythmically and with regard to rhyme)

idiom of "ta'en up wi't." Ta'en up wi' *what*? Everything?
But literally *everything*?

There is of course no single word in such a poem that is
not familiar to a reader with just a slight knowledge of
Scots songs and ballads, and this is true of quite a
number of MacDiarmid's early lyrics, some of which
appeared in the *Glasgow Herald* as well as in his own
periodicals before being collected in *Sangschaw* (1925)
and *Penny Wheep* (1926). These volumes showed conclusively that he could achieve much greater conviction
of style when he used Scots, whether thickly or thinly,
than when he used English. This has to do above all with
rhythm (although it concerns imagery too, as has been
indicated), and it is a matter of feeling rather than think-
ing; for "a thought expressed in a different language may
be practically the same thought, but a feeling or emotion
expressed in a different language is not the same feeling
or emotion."[22]

The confidence that comes of having found a style is
seen as clearly as anywhere in "The Innumerable
Christ" (*Sangschaw*), where the language is a simple colloquial Scots mixed with English, in the sense that sometimes an English word is used although MacDiarmid
must have been familiar with its Scots equivalent, which
is what often happens in actual spoken Scots nowadays.
The idea from which the poem began—a speculative
idea, as are most of the ideas that deeply concern
MacDiarmid—is given in the epigraph from J. Y.
Simpson: "Other stars may have their Bethlehem, and
their Calvary too."

> Wha kens on whatna Bethlehems
> Earth twinkles like a star *a*the nicht,   *a* tonight
> An' whatna shepherds lift their heids
>   In its unearthly licht?
>
> 'Yont a' the stars oor *a*een can see   *a* eyes
> An' farther than their lichts can fly,

I' mony an ^bunco warl' the nicht   ^b unknown world
   The fatefu' bairnies cry.

I' mony an unco warl' the nicht
The ^alift gaes black as pitch at noon,   ^a sky
An' sideways on their chests the ^bheids ^b heads
   O' endless Christs roll doon.

An' when the earth's as cauld's the mune
An' a' its folk are lang syne ^adeid,   ^a dead
On coontless stars the Babe ^bmaun cry ^b must
   An' the Crucified maun bleed.[23]

Any reader who feels that this is just English with a
"Scotch" accent may try for himself the experiment of
putting it into such "standard English" as MacDiarmid
might have used at the time. The following lines, from
MacDiarmid's "Water of Life," may be helpful to him
in the experiment:

> Thy name is Legion, Son of Man,
> And every day is Christmas Day
> And every morn is Easter Morn.
> Where'er the Tides of Life are borne
> You tread upon the waters still.
> You speak to them and they are wine.
> You crave them in Your agony
> And shameful vinegar is Thine, *etc, etc*.[24]

The clue is in the "etc, etc." MacDiarmid in English was
inclined to go floating off on the rhetorical Waters of Life
because of a hollowness, a lack of emotional conviction,
not in what he was saying but in the way he was saying it.

Such a fundamental problem is never finally "solved"
for a poet; he shows the development of which he is
capable in the course of a continual struggle with it.
Therefore MacDiarmid "solved" nothing by changing
from English to Scots. But he did definitely help himself
to come to terms with the problem. His Scots verse is

"more simple, sensuous, and passionate" in "The Innumerable Christ" than anything he had written in
English, partly because the very act of writing in Scots
was an act of faith that heightened emotional commit-
ment and clarified perspective, and partly because it
disencumbered his mind of echoes of all but a very few
other writers. He had much less to forget, and he had
fewer second thoughts, because from the start he had to
entrust more to feeling. These are not unmixed blessings,
but one cannot but be impressed by the increased power
of attack that comes from his seeing his objective more
clearly, the sureness as to rhythm, and the consequences
of the simple but profound fact that, to a Scotsman at least,
Scots is a much more virile language than English.

This brings to mind the sort of grim frankness about
sexual matters that is common to the ballads and to
several of MacDiarmid's early Scots poems, though it is
most obvious in *A Drunk Man Looks at the Thistle*, which
comes slightly later. It is not by any means a grimness
that excludes humour, and in both MacDiarmid and the
ballads it passes without selfconsciousness into the lyric
cry of romantic love poetry. In addition to this, and to the
other ballad influences mentioned earlier, a tough,
masculine terseness may be noted, and along with it an
ability to see drama in ordinary things rather than as
something specially put on for the occasion.

There is also in these poems a delight in the grotesque
and in the life of animals which from one point of view
may be seen as medieval in spirit; a familiarity with God
which used to be the special preserve of Scottish ministers
(the writers being sent to the Devil for congenial company); and a kirkyard humour, specialising in the Resur-
rection, that is a familiar part of popular tradition in
Scotland. We pass rapidly from a bird's eye view ("Whip-
The-World") to an animal's eye view ("Farmer's
Death") to a moon's ("Au Clair de la Lune"), an idiot's
("Jimsy"), a God's ("In the Pantry"), and so on. The

variety is inclined to be more in the changing points of view than in the situations, which are sometimes merely verbal in conception, this last being the weak side of what is only MacDiarmid's strength when he has the imaginative resources to give the words sufficient work to do.

In *Penny Wheep*, as compared with the earlier collection *Sangschaw*, he is less concerned about the company his best poems keep, and there are too many poems that were made to jump out of the dictionary into the cosmos by essentially the same conjuring trick. "Blind Man's Luck" is an example of what I mean. In Jamieson's dictionary, the expression "oon eggs" (eggs laid without the shell; addled eggs) is illustrated by a quotation from an historical drama on Mary Stuart: "O how he turn'd up the whites o' his een [eyes], like twa oon eggs." MacDiarmid's poem follows:

He juist sits *a*oolin' owre the fire	*a* crouching
And *b*gin a body speak t' him, *c*fegs,	*b* if *c* faith!
Turns up the whites o's een	
Like twa oon eggs.	
"I've *a*riped the *b*bike o' Heaven," quo' he,	*a* ransacked
"And whaur ma sicht s'ud be I've stuck	*b* (wasps')
The *c*toom doups o' the sun	nest
And mune, for luck!"[25]	*c* empty bottoms

MacDiarmid could do that sort of thing with such ease that there was a danger of its becoming a formula. However, he had the good sense to see this for himself, and even before the first collection, *Sangschaw*, was completed, he had begun in a longer poem, "The Ballad of the Five Senses," to try something different in Scots. This poem reveals no particular concern with the peculiarities of the Scottish language, no special emphasis on the mere vocabulary that distinguishes it from southern English. But if English seems even slightly foreign to any Scotsman who is sensitive to the subtleties of language—as it

certainly did seem foreign to one of its greatest masters,
the Irishman Joyce—then when he follows a line of
thought in standard English words he is at least to that
extent altering his personality, no matter how thoroughly
he has trained himself to think "in" English. A Scotsman
should think with a Scottish accent, just as he speaks
English with a Scottish accent—unless of course it is his
aim to identify himself with the English, which is all right
for those with nothing else to identify themselves with.

If we were to discount differences in pronunciation
and the tendency to eliminate unimportant consonants,
the language of the "Ballad of the Five Senses" would not
be so very different from southern English. In that case,
what advantage did it offer MacDiarmid? The answer
seems to be that it allowed him to pursue a metaphysical
line of thought without the shift in the gearing of personality required of him by southern English. Such a gear-
change may be barely noticeable in prose; it is of much
more account in the finer mechanism of verse.

Whatever we choose to call it, the linguistic medium
used in the poem adequately sustains an intense movement of thought. And here the movement is carried beyond the last buoys and beacons of the senses to where
pure mind must find within itself "latitude and longitude
on the oceans of speculation" and somehow smuggle
messages back to headquarters. The "Ballad" is indeed a
counterpart in Scots to "A Moment in Eternity." The
differences in style are significant, but this is not the place
for a detailed analysis of two long and in some respects
difficult poems. Perhaps the most fundamental difference
becomes clear if one tries the experiment of removing the
adjectives from the two poems. The reader can no doubt
make a good guess as to the result.

One of the unexpected things about the "Ballad of the
Five Senses" is the use of the old ballad measure for such
a metaphysical subject. Another surprise, when the poem
first appeared, must have been the subtle kinship between

the MacDiarmid revealed in it and the Donne of such poems as "A Nocturnal Upon St Lucy's Day," in which use is made of definition by negatives and similes of difference instead of the customary likeness. Appropriately enough, and with a fine touch of irony, it was in the "Ballad" that George Russell ("Æ") found the lines that made him feel for a moment that MacDiarmid and he had been "born under the same star," although "I soon found that the circle of our beings intersected only at that one point, and, instead of the attraction of affinities, I began to feel the attraction which opposites have for us":[26]

> [a]Leevin' quo' I and [b]deid quo' I,   [a] living   [b] dead
> But daith may only be
> A change o' senses so's a man
> Anither warl' can see.
>
> Or this warl' in anither way
> For Heaven or Hell may be
> But ither ways o' seein' the warl'
> That ony man can see.
>
> And God Himsel' sall only be
> As far's a man can tell,
> In this or ony ither life
> A way o' lookin' at himsel'.[27]

In *Penny Wheep*, along with the second batch of short lyrics in the style that had already become so emphatically his own, MacDiarmid published three longer poems which made much more extensive use of native Scots resources than the "Ballad" had done in developing a medium for sustained thought. The medium is "synthetic" in the sense that it synthesises not only Scots dialect expressions and ancient and current usage but also many elements of southern English. It is something created by MacDiarmid for his own purposes and, though its prevailing current comes from genuine Scottish speech, it is not a linguistic entity to be labelled The

Language of Scotland. As MacDiarmid was to say, in a
bitter mood, and forgetting about Gaelic:

> God gied man speech and speech created thocht,
> He gied man speech but to the Scots gied nocht
> Barrin' this *clytach that they've never   *a* babytalk,
>   brocht   balderdash
> To onything but sic a Blottie O
> As some bairn's copybook micht show.[28]

The first of these longer poems, "Sea Serpent," specu-
lates upon the possibilities of the human mind attaining
an awareness of life as it was when it issued fresh from the
mind of God. It is an impressive achievement, building
up to an invocation of the primitive serpent in which the
poet gathers together the great elemental antitheses in
the most majestic lines heard in Scots verse for four
centuries:

> O Thou that we'd fain be *ane wi' again   *a* one
> Frae the weary lapses o' self set free,
> Be to oor lives as life is to Daith,
> And lift and licht us eternally.
> Frae the *b*howe o' the sea to the *c*heich o' the *d*lift,
> To the licht as licht to the darkness is,   *b* hollow
> Spring fresh and fair frae the spirit o' God   *c* height
> Like the a'e first thocht that He kent was His.   *d* sky

> *a*Loup again in His brain, O Nerve,   *a* leap
> Like a trumpet-stang,
> Lichtnin-clear as when first owre Chaos
> Your shape you flang
> —And *b*swee his mind till the mapamound,   *b* sway
> And meanin' o' ilka man,
> *c*Brenn as then wi' the instant pooer   *c* burn
> O' an only plan![29]

"Bombinations of a Chimera" is a set of variations,
somewhat similar in spirit to Blake's *Proverbs of Hell*, on

the paradoxical theme that Evil must ultimately be good

> Sin' God has cherished us
> Wi' carefu' cruelty,[30]

and therefore should not be resisted by man. The author emerges from the nuptials of Heaven and Hell as "fu' o' elation" as Blake with his "Every thing that lives is Holy."

The third of the longer poems, "Gairmscoile," is not philosophical as the other two are, nor does speculative thought dominate the poem. It begins with a powerful and vivid evocation of the brute nature of man; passes from primitive sex to primitive language, these being seen as intimately linked; suggests that the key to "the spirit of the race" is to be found in the elemental basis of language; encompasses several literary allusions (particularly to Wergeland, the champion of the *Landsmaal* movement in Norway); and ends with a vitriolic flyting in the manner of Dunbar, castigating three unfortunate Scottish versifiers who apparently had indicated their disapproval of MacDiarmid's experiments with Scots.[31] Both the flyting and the allusiveness had been banished from Scots verse for many a long day, and MacDiarmid brought them back in no uncertain fashion. With regard to the allusions, it may be found useful to know that the fourth and fifth lines of section II are an adaptation of Wergeland's statement that

> Most people are good-natured nincompoops,
> hating no one but him that would awaken them;

and the reference to Pegasus being a crocodile and to the poet's mistaking a swamp for the sky come from an insulting address "To Henrik Wergeland" written anonymously by a rival poet and critic, J. S. Welhaven, in *Morganbladet*, 15 Aug. 1830.[32] The other allusions, to G. K. Chesterton's poem "The Donkey" and Francis

D

Jamme's "Lorsqu'il faudra aller vers vous, ô mon Dieu,"
present little difficulty. What they all add up to is an
intimation that MacDiarmid was quite prepared to do in
Scots verse something similar to what T. S. Eliot had
recently been doing with certain allusions in *The Waste
Land*.[33]

Mention of Wergeland conjures up a host of linguistic
and literary revivals that might provide partial analogies
for the case of Scots. However, the apathy of much of
Scotland towards political nationalism weakens most of
the analogies, and it seems better to avoid them also because they tend to put theoretical considerations between
the reader and the poet's actual practice, which is of
primary concern here. MacDiarmid certainly knew about
Ivan Aasen and his *Grammar of the Popular Language of
Norway*—he made it his business to know about such
things—but he did not compile a Scots grammar; he
wrote a poem alluding to Pegasus as a crocodile. Simi-
larly, in theory, MacDiarmid declared that the linguistic
problem confronting the writer of Scots was "to determine what 'motor-car' would have been in the Doric had
the Doric continued, or, rather, become an all-sufficient
independent language."[34] But forty years later we are still
beguiling the time by reading his poems while waiting
for an answer.

Even in these poems, the reader should beware of
regarding as the whole truth any statement made by
MacDiarmid about the nature of his experiments, because he is quite liable to adopt contradictory points of
view at different times—and not seldom at one and the
same time. "Gairmscoile" is a case in point, for at the
very moment when he was engaged in what he called the
intellectualisation of Scots verse, he was declaring in this
poem that

> *It's soond, no' sense, that faddoms the herts o' men.*
> *And by my sangs the ᵃrough auld Scots I ken*   ᵃ rough

> *E'en herts that ha'e nae Scots'll* ^b*dirl richt thro'*   ^b thrill
> *As nocht else could—for here's a language rings*
> *Wi'* ^c*datchie sesames, and names for nameless*   ^c cunning,
> *things.*[35]   secret

And he was using the sophisticated literary allusions already referred to as support for his claims for the *primitive* qualities of his language:

> Mony's the auld half-human cry I ken
> Fa's like a revelation on the herts o' men
> As tho' the graves were split and the first man
> Grippit the latest wi' a freendly han'.
> ... And there's forgotten shibboleths o' the Scots
> Ha'e keys to senses lockit to us yet
> —Coorse words that shamble thro' oor minds like
>   ^astots,   ^a bullocks
> Syne turn on's muckle een wi' doonsin' emerauds lit.[36]

There is here the essence both of J. M. Synge's view that "before verse can be human again it must learn to be brutal,"[37] and of Robert Frost's attempt to "write down certain brute noises so that no one could miss them in my sentences. I have counted on doubling the meaning of my sentences with them."[38]

With MacDiarmid one finds that one is always returning to questions of *language*. Indeed it is this factor that holds his whole life's work together as perhaps nothing else does. Therefore, before passing on to what is generally agreed to be his masterpiece, the book-length poem *A Drunk Man Looks at the Thistle* (1926), it may be useful to summarise in his own words, as they are to be found in early editorials and essays, those aspects of the Scots language that were most relevant to his purposes. There appear to be four of these, more or less distinguishable, though closely linked together.

(*a*) *Psychological.* "From this point of view, the value of the Doric lies in the extent to which it contains lapsed or unrealised qualities which correspond to 'unconscious' elements of distinctively Scottish psychology."[39]

(b) *Moral*. The use of standard English imposes a puritanical censorship on the writer. Joyce, an Irishman making his approach from outside the main English tradition, had tried to break through this censorship; and "we have been enormously struck by the resemblance—the moral resemblance—between Jamieson's *Etymological Dictionary of the Scottish Language* and James Joyce's *Ulysses*. A *vis comica* that has not yet been liberated lies bound by desuetude and misappreciation in the recesses of the Doric: and its potential uprising would be no less prodigious uncontrollable, and utterly at variance with conventional morality than was Joyce's tremendous outpouring."[40]

(c) *Logopoeic and Onomatopoeic*. "Another feature of the Doric . . . is the fashion in which diverse attitudes of mind or shades of temper are telescoped into single words or phrases, investing the whole speech with subtle flavours of irony, commiseration, realism and humour which cannot be reproduced in English. In onomatopoeic effect, too, the Doric has a wider range and infinitely richer resources than English. . . ."[41]

(d) *Aesthetic*. "One of the most distinctive characteristics of the Vernacular, part of its very essence, is its insistent recognition of the body, the senses. . . . This explains the unique blend of the lyrical and the ludicrous in primitive Scots sentiment. . . . The essence of the genius of our race is, in our opinion, the reconciliation it effects between the base and the beautiful, recognising that they are complementary and indispensable to each other."[42]

"The unique blend of the lyrical and the ludicrous"; "the reconciliation between the base and the beautiful." This leads us to an idea that is of prime importance to an understanding of MacDiarmid's work as a whole and which offers an illuminating approach to *A Drunk Man Looks at the Thistle*. He came across the idea in Gregory Smith's *Scottish Literature: Character and Influence* (1919)

and put it to such extensive use that it has passed with
every appearance of inevitability into two of the latest
studies of the subject: Sydney Goodsir Smith's *Short
Introduction to Scottish Literature* (1951) and Kurt Wittig's
Scottish Tradition in Literature (1958). Gregory Smith's line
of thought may be picked out as follows:

> Perhaps in the very combination of opposites—what
> either of the two Sir Thomases, of Norwich and
> Cromarty, might have been willing to call 'the Cale-
> donian Antisyzygy'—we have a reflection of the con-
> trasts which the Scot shows at every turn. . . . Though
> the Scottish Muse has loved reality, sometimes to
> maudlin affection for the commonplace, she has loved
> not less the airier pleasure to be found in the confusion
> of the senses, in the fun of things thrown topsyturvy, in
> the horns of elfland and the voices of the mountains.
> . . . There is more in the Scottish antithesis of the real
> and fantastic than is to be explained by the familiar
> rules of rhetoric. The sudden jostling of contraries
> seems to preclude any relationship by literary sug-
> gestion. The one invades the other without warning.
> They are the 'polar twins' of the Scottish Muse.[43]

The "Caledonian Antisyzygy" is never far from
MacDiarmid's mind in *A Drunk Man Looks at the Thistle*—
lines such as "Grinning gargoyle by a saint" come straight
from Gregory Smith—and it is this conception of the
Scottish Muse that is celebrated in the poem. Behind
Gregory Smith we may discern Coleridge's perception
that the Imagination reveals itself in "the balance or
reconciliation of opposite or discordant qualities";[44] and
lurking round the corner is Samuel Johnson with his
definition of Wit as "a kind of *discordia concors*; a combination of dissimilar images, or discovery of occult re-
semblances in things apparently unlike."[45] "Of wit, thus
defined," as Johnson said of the seventeenth-century
metaphysical poets, MacDiarmid had "more than

enough"; and it was by this apparently roundabout route that certain characteristics of *A Drunk Man* fitted in with the contemporary revival of interest in Donne and the other metaphysicals. In fact, an anonymous writer (perhaps William Power) in the *Scots Observer* for 2 Jul. and 5 Nov. 1927, referred to MacDiarmid as "a Doric Donne"; and although the adjective is unfortunate in its associations, the perception was acute. It is more difficult to show the connexion between *A Drunk Man* and "the poetry of Trakl and other little-known German poets I like for the sake of a certain Gothicity, or the rôle of *grotesquerie* in revitalizing phases of literature";[46] but there *is* a connexion, and some day a literary historian will give us a detailed account of the kinship between MacDiarmid and Arno Holz, some of whose work he knew at any rate in translation by this time.

Most important of all, the antisyzygical conception of the Scottish Muse allowed MacDiarmid to identify his interest in the psychology of the creative process, especially in so far as he could analyse it within himself, with his search for the "genius," the psychological "quiddity" of his own people, so that in the last analysis the roots of the Thistle are found in the mind of the Drunk Man:

> For a' that's Scottish is in me . . .
> And I in turn 'ud be an action
> To pit in a concrete abstraction
> My country's contrair qualities
> And mak' a unity of these.[47]

MacDiarmid has pushed the Caldeonian Antisyzygy to the point of mania, evidently on Blake's principle that "you never know what is enough unless you know what is more than enough";[48] but to begin with it was what he described as a *point fixé*:

Most omnivorous readers know how curiously any theme that impresses itself upon them will run through all their subsequent reading until another supplants it; how everything one reads at such a time will throw some new light or yield some additional information, or bear in this way or that on that *point fixé*.[49]

The two brightest lights were thrown by Dostoevsky and Léon Chestov, and are most clearly reflected in these lines:

> I'll ha'e nae hauf-way hoose, but aye be
>   whaur
> Extremes meet—it's the only way I ken
> To dodge the curst conceit o' bein' richt
> That damns the vast majority o' men.[50]

None of the commentaries on *A Drunk Man* appear to take these two influences very seriously, but they clearly meant a great deal to MacDiarmid at the time. A whole section of the poem was originally called "Homage to Dosto-evsky,"[51] in relation to whom MacDiarmid described himself, with a modesty he rarely allows to appear in print, as a "bairn" to a "giant." Most of the Christ references and the idea of being "fu' o' a stickit God" cannot be properly understood except in relation to "the titanic Russian"; while it was Chestov ("my favourite philosopher," "my master") who took MacDiarmid over "that frontier beyond which the might of general ideas ceases" to "try his luck with the idea of chaos."[52] And it was another Russian philosopher, Soloviev, whose con-ception of Sophia, the Wisdom of God, he adopted as the unifying element amongst the "seemingly irreconcilable qualities" of human experience. In the light of the Cale-donian Antisyzygy, it is significant that Soloviev used "le terme interéssant de 'syzygie', signifiant la réunion des aspects réel et idéal du monde, du principe actif per-sonnel et de l'idée une et totale."[53]

The title, *A Drunk Man Looks at the Thistle*, was supplied by MacDiarmid's friend and former teacher, the com-poser F. G. Scott. We have the authority of Maurice

Lindsay for the story that Scott, who had been making
musical settings of many of MacDiarmid's poems, received a telegram in Glasgow and rushed to Montrose,
where he found the poet "surrounded by innumerable
bits of paper, 'about six inches long', on which were
written the lyrics out of which the poem was finally made
up. According to Scott, there was no arrangement about
the squares of paper." The aid of a bottle of whisky was
invoked and after some hours of picking and choosing
they "got the thing into order," and Scott thought up the
brilliant stroke of giving the last word to the protagonist's
wife, after MacDiarmid had come to an end with the line
"O I ha'e silence left":

> —"And weel ye micht,"
> Sae Jean'll say, efter sic a nicht!"[54]

To this diverting anecdote must be added the fact that
six samples of a poem already called *A Drunk Man Looks
at the Thistle*, and described as "a complete poem, *in over
600 lines*, deriving its unity from its preoccupation with
the distinctive elements in Scottish psychology which
depend for their effective expression upon the hitherto
unrealised potentialities of Braid Scots," appeared in the
Glasgow Herald for 13 Feb. 1926. And these extracts,
although self-contained, clearly present the same key-
symbols that are developed throughout the poem as published, *in about 2,500 lines*, in November of that year. Also
it should be remembered that MacDiarmid himself
when confessing his "inartistry" and his consequent great
debt to Scott, said of the latter's help with the *Drunk Man*
manuscript that "he was not long in seizing on the essen-
tials and urging the ruthless discarding of the unessen-
tials."[55] This is a very different matter from there being
"no arrangement about the squares of paper."

"Criticism of its meaning is forestalled by the title and
the ironic preface," said the *Times Literary Supplement*
reviewer when the book appeared;[56] and he has been

echoed ever since, though there have been mercifully fewer echoes of his further dictum that "it is idle to attempt a coherent account of a poem so deliberately and provocatively incoherent." As a matter of fact, as David Daiches has indicated in his excellent introduction to the second edition,[57] the poem is remarkable for the absence of the obscurity that pervades the verse of so many of MacDiarmid's contemporaries, and its discursive parts, far from being "so much padding," provide "its logic and its dramatic unity." But the "Author's Note" to the poem as first published, which has been restored in the third edition,[58] was and is a mistake. By defending himself in advance, MacDiarmid made prejudice a present of ammunition, some of which it would have been too lazy to find for itself. He began by calling the poem a "gallimaufry," and proceeded to warn sober readers against any attempt to confer "a species of intelligibility foreign to its nature upon my poem," since "drunkeness has a logic of its own."

A sympathetic critic, William Soutar, saw this as at best "a brilliant manoeuvre by which he shifts the onus of responsibility upon his readers"; and Soutar granted only "a semblance of consistency . . . a consistency of emotional tone," to the work as a whole.[59] But it has much more than that. The key-symbols of Thistle and Rose, Moon and Woman, Whisky and Sea-Serpent, are fecund themes on which imagination and fancy alike play variations with a flow of figurative invention unequalled by any other modern poet; and they have a staying-power that ensures that the themes are not lost in the brilliance of the invention. It is true that there is a dangerous extempore quality about the technique of the author, who permits himself a carelessness in some details that would stick out like sore thumbs against the more sophisticated texture of standard English, but (changing the hounds in chase of a very elusive quarry) he does achieve a triumphant if precarious balance between the "twin poles of the Scottish Muse."

Burns, Dostoevsky, Melville and Christ—along with lesser figures like Jekyll and Hyde, Masoch and Sade, Deosil and Widdershins, and of course Cyclone and Anti —have all been partners of MacDiarmid's Jean in the cosmic dance, and at the heart of the poem there is a deeply honest scrutiny of the connexion between human sexuality and the creation of poetry, morality, and religion:

> I wish I kent the physical basis
> O' a' life's seemin' airs and graces.

> It's queer the thochts a *a*kittled cull   *a* tickled testicle
> Can lowse or *b*splairgin' glit annul.[60]   *b* splattering slime

The *vis comica* of the Scots has its uprising at last, and its liberation is no less violently shocking than MacDiarmid had forecast: but the thistle that is seen as a phallus is also seen as the tree of Yggdrasil, binding together heaven and earth and hell, and much that is in between them.

A Drunk Man is one of the great poems of modern times. Without quite bursting at the seams, it is able to hold all or almost all of MacDiarmid—which is to say that it is crammed full of fine lyrics, satire, flyting, parody, burlesque, occasional verse, Rabelaisian jokes, metaphysical conceits, translations and adaptations, sustained meditations and speculations on philosophical and religious problems, elemental symbols, and allusions recondite and otherwise. The vehicle for all this is a dramatic monologue which presents us with a stream of consciousness, but the consciousness is a creative one, passing from memory to reflexion, from sense-impressions to metaphysical speculations, and seeking to interpret to itself its own flux in terms of analogy and metaphor, symbol and myth. The ultimate subject of the work is the creative process itself, as though the author were showing us what came before and after and between his separate poems, as well as these poems themselves. The result will not be random if the author really does have sufficient depth and strength of imagination, the Coleridgian "esemplastic power" that is not independent of the will and understanding but is "retained under their irremissive, though gentle and unnoticed control, *laxis effertur haberis*."[61] But obviously it must stand or fall by the quality of the mind that is here revealed in its entirety without benefit of the formal insulation of self-contained works of art. And it does stand—dangerously balanced but magnificent. For the quality of mind that supports it has a speculative stamina that carries the reader with it from Scotland through the Waste Land of Europe to the Chestovian Abyss and back—and ends with a joke.

A poem of such length must alternate between higher and lower pitches of intensity, and it is the less intense passages that must sustain our interest in the whole. It was here that MacDiarmid's powers were most crucially tested and finally vindicated. His willingness to explore all the side-streets and back-lanes as well as the main avenues of thought and feeling, together with his frequent changes of pace, make it impossible to characterise any part of the work as "pedestrian" in the derogatory sense. And when he does follow a main avenue, and one begins to feel one is quite familiar with all this, he will take one unerringly that extra bit further than one has ever been before.

When not deeply imaginative—as who can be all the time?—he has astonishing resources of metaphysical wit and satirical, fantastic, or grotesque humour at his command. Wit in the sense that Donne had wit, a mental and emotional and verbal agility in juggling with the mutations of possibility, permeates the whole poem. We should tire of this if it were mere cleverness, mere sleight of mind, but it is not just that; it is based in a deep and genuine scepticism that scrutinises and tests received

ideas by turning them upside down and inside out and
shaking them hard. When he does this with the pieties of
received religion, some people are unduly shocked and
other people are unduly proud of not being shocked, but
in neither camp are there many who see the important
point that here is the work of a mind much more deeply
concerned with religion than they are, a mind that has
listened to the dripping of the tap of eternity

> And heard God passin' wi' a bobby's feet
> Ootby in the lang coffin o' the street.[62]

The parallel with Joyce is plain to see. But with Donne
too, in his different way, he shares the power of "dis-
solving orient pearls worth a kingdom, in a health to a
whore."

MacDiarmid, like Donne, is a great believer in shock-
tactics, and not everybody cares for his "fine sense of the
value of provocation." But the ironic violence which
David Daiches has said to be the typical characteristic of
A Drunk Man is not just a clashing of symbols, as in so
much modern verse, but a true and strenuous attempt to
break down the partitions between "all the rooms of
life," since "watertight compartments are useful only to a
sinking ship."[63] There are many people who insist on
having other rooms besides the living-room, and it is not
surprising that some of MacDiarmid's shock-tactics
should have been regarded as awful examples of bad
taste. But it is arguable that poetry, especially English
poetry, has had far too much quiet good taste for its own
good.

We could well do without the author's advertisement
of his own genius in A Drunk Man, but this is too obstin-
ately rooted to be wished out of the poem. It is there, it is
undoubtedly an aesthetic flaw, but a poem can be flawed
and still have greatness; and part of the greatness of this
one comes in the end from the suffering that the assumption of genius must cause:

Ha'e I the cruelty I need,
Contempt and syne contempt o' that,
And still contempt in endless meed
That I may never yet be caught
In ony satisfaction, or
Bird-lime that winna let me soar?

Bite into me forever mair and lift
Me clear o' chaos in a great relief
Till, like this thistle in the munelicht growin'
I brak in roses owre a hedge o' grief.[64]

We are left at the last with the thistle, beside which the symbols of other poets look small. In MacDiarmid's eyes, it is everything from the aborted child of Scotland, half soul and half skeleton, to coloured ping-pong balls on water jets at a shooting gallery, or a company of Highland soldiers swallowed by alligators with nothing but the pompons of their Balmoral bonnets left to tell the tale, or Yggdrasil uniting man and the infinite. To give a fair picture of its scope one would have to quote page after page of the book. In the circumstances, it seems best to take the author's hint:

Yet ha'e I Silence left, the [a]croon o' a'.   [a] crown

No' her, wha on the hills langsyne I saw
Liftin' a foreheid o' perpetual snaw.

No' her, wha in the how-dumb-deid o' nicht
[a]Kyths, like Eternity in Time's despite.   [a] appears

No' her, withooten shape, wha's name is
      Daith,
No' Him, unkennable [b]abies to faith   [b] except

—God who, gin e'er He saw a man, 'ud be
E'en mair dumfooner'd at the sicht than he.

　　—But Him, whom nocht in man or Deity,
Or Daith or Dreid or Laneliness can touch,
Wha's ^cdeed owre often and has seen owre much.　　　*^c died*

O I ha'e Silence left.[65]

REFERENCES

1. "Parnassus and Schiehallion are one," "Valedictory," *N.N.*, 2nd Series, p. 55.
2. *S.C.*, Aug. 1922, p. 4.
3. P. Geddes, "The Scots Renascence," *E.*, Spring 1895, pp. 131–9. C. M. Grieve, "A Theory of Scots Letters," *S.C.*, Feb. 1923, p. 181–4. D. Saurat, "Le Groupe de 'La Renaissance écossaise'," *R.A.*, Apr. 1924.
4. The name Nisbet was probably suggested by the memory of John Bogue Nisbet, a young poet friend who was killed at Loos. (Cp. *Lycidas*.)
5. *S.C.*, Aug. & Sep. 1922, pp. 15–19, 46–50.
6. *S.C.*, Aug. 1922, p. iii.
7. Sydney Goodsir Smith was to follow up this hint a quarter of a century later with *Carotid Cornucopius*, Glasgow 1947, a "badside buik" in which some of the pyrotechnics of *Finnegans Wake* are exploded under Arthur's Seat, or thereabouts.
8. "The Watergaw," *S.C.*, Oct. 1922. *C.P.*, p. 7.
9. "Causerie," *S.C.*, Oct. 1922.
10. *L.P.*, p. xiii.
11. *S.C.*, Dec. 1922, p. 122.
12. *S.*, p. 23 (17).
13. *L.P.*, p. 65.
14. "Holie for Nags," *S.O.*, 22 Sep. 1928, p. 5.
15. "Genethliacon for the New World Order," *S.L.*, p. 42.
16. *D.M.*, p. 68 (126).
17. *S.*, p. 35 (22).
18. *S.*, p. 12 (12).
19. *P.W.*, p. 50 (50).
20. In an address to the Scottish Association for the Speaking of Verse on 12 Mar. 1958.
21. *Ancient and Modern Scots Songs* (1st edn.), p. 109.
22. T. S. Eliot, "The Social Function of Poetry," in *On Poetry and Poets*, London 1957, pp. 15–25.
23. *S.*, pp. 33–4 (21–2).
24. *N.N.*, 3rd Series, pp. 56–7.
25. *P.W.*, p. 4 (31).
26. "Introductory Essay," in *1st H.*, pp. 1–6.
27. "Ballad of the Five Senses," in *S.*, pp. 43–52 (25–9).
28. *D.M.*, p. 37 (99).
29. "Sea Serpent," in *P.W.*, pp. 11–15 (33–6).
30. "Bombinations of a Chimera," *P.W.*, pp. 38–45 (45–8).
31. For the record, they were Gilbert Rae of Biggar, John Smellie Martin of Motherwell, and John J.

Sutherland, author of *Aiberdeen an' Twal' Mile Roon'*.

32. See I. Grøndhal & O. Raknes, *Chapters in Norwegian Literature*, London 1923, p. 58.

33. "Gairmscoile," as published in *P.W.*, consists of the Prologue and Sections I and II of a long poem planned to have twelve Sections and an Epilogue. The third Section and the titles of the others are given in *S.C.*, Nov.–Dec. 1923.

34. "Causerie," *S.C.*, Oct. 1922.

35. *P.W.*, pp. 68–9 (58).

36. *P.W.*, pp. 67–8 (57).

37. J. M. Synge, "Preface" to *Poems and Translations*, Dublin 1912, pp. xi–xii.

38. Quoted by J. Isaacs in "Best Loved American Poet," in *The Listener*, Apr. 1954, p. 566.

39. "Causerie," *S.C.*, Oct. 1922, p. 63.

40. "A theory of Scots Letters—I," in *S.C.*, Feb. 1922, p. 183.

41. "A theory of Scots Letters—II," *S.C.*, Mar. 1922, p. 212.

42. "A theory of Scots Letters—I," *S.C.*, Feb. 1922, p. 184.

43. *Op. cit.*, pp. 4, 19, 20.

44. *Biographia Literaria* (Everyman edn.), London 1947, p. 151.

45. *Lives of the Most Eminent English Poets*, London (F. Wayne & Co.) n.d., p. 9.

46. *L.P.*, pp. 46–7.

47. *D.M.*, p. 71 (129).

48. W. Blake, *Poems* (ed. L. Binyon), London 1931, p. 163.

49. "Causerie," in *N.R.*, p. 3.

50. *D.M.*, p. 6 (67).

51. *G.H.*, 13 Feb. 1926, p. 4.

52. *L.P.*, pp. 40, 67.

53. B. Zenkovsky, *Histoire de la philosophie russe*, Paris 1954, Vol. 2, p. 50. For MacDiarmid's interest in Soloviev, see *G.H.*, 17 Mar. 1923, p. 6, and *S.C.*, Jul. 1923, p. 354.

54. "Talking with F. G. Scott," *S.R.*, Winter 1954, pp. 48–55.

55. *F.G.S.*, p. 24.

56. *T.L.S.*, 22 Sep. 1927, pp. 650–1.

57. *D.M.*, Glasgow 1953, pp. xiii–xx.

58. *D.M.*, Edinburgh 1956, pp. vii–viii.

59. "The Poetry of Hugh MacDiarmid," *F.M.*, 7 Apr. 1934, pp. 8–9.

60. *D.M.*, p. 22 (83).

61. *Biographia Literaria* (Everyman edn.), p. 151.

62. *D.M.*, p. 73 (130).

63. *L.P.*, p. 333.

64. *D.M.*, pp. 71, 34 (128, 96).

65. *D.M.*, p. 96 (150–1).

CHAPTER IV

SNAKES AND LADDERS

When Blackwood's brought out *A Drunk Man* in November 1926, they advertised a new book "in preparation" called *To Circumjack Cencrastus*; but four years were to go by before this second long poem-sequence was in fact published. Growing frustration with his job in Montrose, followed by the disastrous moves to London and Liverpool, made it increasingly difficult for MacDiarmid to come to grips with his theme, which had been suggested by a letter from Lascelles Abercrombie, who told him: "You have a serpent in you which will eat up everything else." This was associated in the poet's memory with a winding path near Langholm called the Curly Snake, of which he says: "It has always haunted my imagination and has probably constituted itself the ground-plan and pattern of my mind. . . ."[1]

The serpent's name was Cencrastus, and he crawled out of James Watson's *Choice Collection* (1709), where he was described as "a beist of filthy braith," and reached MacDiarmid via Jamieson's *Dictionary*. The latter also provided the verb "to circumjack" (*circumjacere*—to lie round or about), which MacDiarmid used in a special sense to accord with the ancient Gaelic saying, "It's a big beast there's no room for outside." The general idea seems to have been that, instead of the snake eating him, he would eat the snake.

"The general idea"—because, unfortunately, it remained something general, vague, and unrealised in the book when *To Circumjack Cencrastus* finally appeared in 1930. The snake is active only at long intervals, tantalisingly but ineffectively, and when an attempt is made near the end of the book to stitch in a symbolism of sea and serpent, one observes that this should have been taken care of at the planning stage.

It is true of *Cencrastus* in a pejorative sense of the term not really applicable to *A Drunk Man* that it is a "gallimaufry." Or, changing the figure, it lacks a centre of gravity, so that its parts go flying off in all directions, like a spiritualist séance in a gale.

One feels, not so much that MacDiarmid has lost his power, but rather that he has lost his grip. There are excellent original things in the book but, equally with the adaptation of Rilke and the reappearance of "A Moment in Eternity," one feels the lack of an assurance that they were placed there with a firm sense of what their author was about. There is in several places an impression of marking time; and then we are offered extempore distractions (sometimes lively, sometimes dull) to keep us occupied while the author searches desperately for something that is on the tip of his mind— a clue to a new rhythm of thought that keeps evading him because

There is nae movement in the warld like yours.

Clearly, this might have been subsumed in the general idea of the elusive serpent, but the fact remains that in terms of art it is not. For example, the problem of *language*, to which the author keeps returning from time to time in the poem, is not linked (as it could so easily be linked) to the serpent tongue of Cencrastus. Yet this problem of language, and the need for a tradition to go with it, is his most insistent theme.

Instead of the serpent, it is "The Mavis of Pabal"[2] that announces this theme. The mavis comes from a Gaelic song by John MacCodrum (translated by John Stuart Blackie), and, metamorphosed into MacDiarmid, the bird regains his place "on the tap o' the hill" where, he says,

E

> ... I'll sing as I sang in the past
> —If singing' depends upon will.

But will is not enough, as MacDiarmid well knows,

> For poetry's no' made in a lifetime
> And I lack a livin' past.

Also, one mavis does not make a renaissance, but

> There's nae sign o' a mate to be seen.

However, as we are told later, *On àird tuaidh tig in chabhair* ("Help comes from the northern airt"), for it is there that the Scottish poet can recover his lost Gaelic background, "get down to *Ur-motives*," and "get back behind the [European] Renaissance."[3] But this involves the problem of language:

> *O wad at least my yokel words*
> *Some Gaelic strain had kept! ...*
>
> Curse on my dooble life and dooble tongue
> —Guid Scots wi' English a' hamstrung—
>
> *Speakin' o' Scotland in English words*
> *As it were Beethoven chirpt by birds.*[4]

There is, for all but a few Scotsmen, a linguistic block between them and their Gaelic *Ur-motives*, and we are not convinced by MacDiarmid's "hauf-English" in this poem that there is still

> Time eneuch ... to seek the Omnific Word
>   In Jamieson yet,
> Or the new Dictionary in the makin' noo,
>   Or coin it oorsels!

Yet it is by going back to the Celtic past, and linking Scotland with Ireland, Cornwall and Wales, that MacDiarmid would take us forward again to a point at which, in his vision, we may

> ... turn to Europe and see
> Hoo the emergence o' the Russian Idea's
> Broken the balance o' the North and Sooth
> And needs a coonter that can only be
>   The Gaelic Idea
> To mak' a parallelogram o' forces,
>   Complete the Defence o' the West,
> And end the English betrayal o' Europe.[5]

Now, a forked-tongued Celtic Snake of Wisdom might help us imaginatively to swallow all this, as it contrives to swallow its own tail, but MacDiarmid's serpent is kept well out of the picture, and he offers only the lame excuse that

> We're no' used to snakes in Scotland here
> And ha'e suffered frae Knox on the heid sae lang
> That we micht tak' a blindworm, or at best
>   An adder, for Cencrastus![6]

Particularly when one remembers MacDiarmid's passionate invocation of the Sea-Serpent in *Penny Wheep*, one cannot but find Cencrastus altogether too negative a concept to form the nexus of a very long poem—a poem of perhaps 4,000 lines—much longer even than *A Drunk Man*. Far from his being an all-persuasive presence, one is rather aware of Cencrastus as something outside the poem, because outside the scope of language itself:

> I was a bard in Alba and Eire, but the Muse
> That I'm concerned wi' noo has heard o'
>   neither,
> And it wad tak' a life as lang's Methuselah's
> For ony Scot or Irishman to ᵃbig   ᵃ build
> Machineries o' expression like the English,
>   French or German
> —That haena circumjacked you yet.[7]

Similarly, when the Muse becomes Valéry's Athikte (Goddess of Measurement), we get only a glimpse of her before she is drowned in the sea,

> *And even the art o' MacDiarmid*
> *Leaves her a ªconnached mermaid.*[8]   ª washed out

There is often a tiredness about the poem, reflected in the language, which is mainly English pronounced *more Boreali*, though the poet says that

> A' this is juist provisional and 'll hae
> A tea-change into something rich and Scots
> When I wha needs use English a' the day
> Win back to the true language o' my thochts.[9]

The complaints about his job, domestic worries, the stupidities of the "vast majority of men" (fast becoming MacDiarmid's favourite phrase) seem almost inevitable. They are the surface signs of a deeper souring of the spirit in the lonely struggle

> To think nae thocht that's e'er been thocht afore
> And nane that's no' worth mair than a' that ha'e,

since

> There's naething that a man can be
> That's mair than imbecile to me
> In the licht o' totality.[10]

But the yeast is there too, bubbling irrepressibly through even the ranklings of the *Montrose Review* reporter's petty indignities at the hands of his boss:

> Curse his new hoose, his business, his cigar,
> His wireless set, and motor car,
> Alsatian, gauntlet gloves, plus fours and wife,
> —A' thing included in his life;
> And, abune a', his hearty laughter,
> And—if he has yin—his hereafter.[11]

And in the middle of the self-conscious blasphemies
directed against "the common God," especially the God
of the Scottish Presbyterian Churches, there appear
amazing lines, lines that no one else could have written:

> And aye the veil is rent and a' I see
> In horror-stricken blasphemy is mysel'
> As in a mirror, and owre my shoulder, Daith,
> And yont Daith Life again—an endless swell
> O' mountain efter mountain, a faithfu' flock
> Each wi' a *a*bawbee for the collection *b*poke![12]   *a* ha'penny
>   *b* pouch

If, *sub specie aeternitatis*, what man has made of life is a
bad joke, MacDiarmid at least tries to make a better joke
of it, and specifically exhorts his compatriots accordingly:

> "Let's mak' a better joke in politics and art
> Than the English yet—and damn consistency!"[13]

Yet his dream of the "Gaelic Idea" has a serious basis, in
Spenglerian terms, in "an effort in every aspect of the
national life to supplant the elements at present pre-
dominant by the other elements they have suppressed,
and thus reverse the existing order."[14] But MacDiarmid
cannot absorb the ethos of Gaeldom with the same ease as
Grieve did that of Lowland Scotland:

> —*Fain through Burns' clay MacMhaighstir's fire*
> *To glint within me aettled.*   *a* aspired
> *It stirred, alas, but couldna bkyth,*   *b* appear
> *Prood, elegant and mettled.*[15]

The lack of structural development in Gaelic poetry,
which makes it so radically different from the main
Western European tradition, was probably a bad influence on MacDiarmid, and although he greatly admired
its technical virtuosity, he was not able to make much of
that kind of technique work *for him*. Taking his bearings
from Daniel Corkery's *Hidden Ireland* (1925), he saw in the

Celtic tradition a way of "getting back behind the Renaissance" to a deeper conception of classicism than Hulme and Eliot had been advocating in their different fashion: but the practical results of this in *Cencrastus* do not go much beyond a tentative "Scots Anthology" *vis-à-vis* the Greek. This is excellent of its kind, but it is a very long way from the "creation of major forms"[16] which MacDiarmid expected (at least as early as 1927) to result from a return to the Gaelic roots of Scotland.

MacDiarmid's knowledge of the Gaelic languages seems to have been based on a bare smattering picked up from a relative in childhood,[17] and the source of his references to and quotations from Irish poets in *Cencrastus* was Aodh de Blácam's *Gaelic Literature Surveyed* (1929). However, there is more to some of the Irish references than may at first be apparent. One of the hottest controversies of the time in Scotland concerned the so-called "Irish Invasion" of the country, which raised religious and political as well as economic issues there, and it is only in that context that one can fully understand MacDiarmid's oblique reference to *Tabhroidh chugam cruit mo ríogh*. This is a poem by Gilbride Albanach MacNamee concerning a treasured Irish harp which somehow found its way to Scotland, where its adopted guardian refused to part with it. It is the latter whose "honey mouth" is blessed by his fellow countryman, MacDiarmid.[18] From MacDiarmid's point of view, "the growth of Catholicism [in Scotland] and the influx of the Irish are alike welcome, as undoing those accompaniments of the Reformation which have lain like a blight on Scottish arts and affairs."[19]

There are hints in *Cencrastus* of another great Idea, in addition to the Gaelic one, that represented for Mac-Diarmid the future role of his people in history: the Social Credit economics of C. H. Douglas (concerning whom it should be remembered that he was a Scotsman, and worked out a "Draft Scheme" for Scotland). But economic changes, unless accompanied by intellectual, psychological and spiritual changes, still seemed to the poet to amount to nothing:

> I'm oot for shorter oors and higher pay
> And better conditions for a' workin' folk
> But ken the hellish state in which they live's
> Due maistly to their ain mob cowardice.
> Yet tho' a' men were millionaires the morn
> > As they could easily be
> They'd be nae better than maist rich folk noo
> And nocht that maitters much 'ud be improved
> > And micht be waur.[20]

Eric Linklater has in one of his novels a description of MacDiarmid ("Hugh Skene") addressing a meeting in Edinburgh to urge the case for Douglas economics: " 'I have no interest whatsoever in prosperity,' he declared, and left the uncommon impression that here was a man who advanced an economic theory for purely aesthetic reasons."[21] If so, the aesthetic he had in mind was no joke:

> To hell wi' happiness!
> I sing the terrifying discipline
> O' the free mind that [a]gars a man   [a] makes
> Mak' his joys kill his joys,
> The weakest by the strongest,
> The temporal by the fundamental
> (Or hope o' the fundamental)
> And prolong wi' in himself
> Threids o' thocht sae fragile
> It needs the help and contrivance
> O' a' his vital poo'er
> To [b]haud them frae brakin'   [b] hold
> As he pu's them owre the gulfs.
> Oor humanity canna follow us
> To lichts sae faur removed.[22]

It is MacDiarmid's preoccupation with the cruelty and mystery of genius that is the link between the title-poem and some of the others in *First Hymn to Lenin and Other*

Poems (1931). And it ought to be linked to these others—
not regarded in isolation, nor yet as part of the trio of
Three Hymns to Lenin (finally published only in 1957),
since this has been known to give the quite wrong impression that the author switched abruptly to a different
kind of poetry, a political poetry designed for proletarian
consumption. The *First Hymn* and the *Second*, which tells
us a great deal more about MacDiarmid's conception of
poetry than it does about politics or Lenin, were intended
to form part of a huge autobiographical poem in five
volumes called *Clann Albann*.[23] They were to be placed in
"The Muckle Toon," the first volume of that never-
completed work, along with the "other poems" of 1931,
the whole of *Scots Unbound and Other Poems* (1932), and
numerous other items that have so far appeared only in
periodicals. Equally with the rest of that volume, they
were associated with Langholm, the poet's birthplace in
Dumfriesshire, and in so far as they have a specifically
political orientation "they are in logical sequence from
the radicalism of that Border burgh" and are "presented
merely as starting points for the attitudes developed from
book to book."[24] But MacDiarmid did not see them as
being primarily political poems; otherwise he would have
placed them in the *second* volume of *Clann Albann* as he
planned it.

Certainly there may have been ulterior motives for
MacDiarmid letting it be known to his critics that "none
of the opinions expressed are necessarily his own at all;
all these poems are part of a big scheme in which the
diverse points of view expressed will be balanced against
each other."[25] But even so, it is a fact that the attitude he
adopted towards Lenin and revolutionary Communism
is best understood if one sees the first two *Hymns* in the
context of the other poems which he was writing at that
time. These show that he was especially preoccupied with
the source of "inspiration" and the mysterious factors that
go to produce "genius," because he believed the hope of

mankind to lie in the possibility of evolving a race of men
to whom what is now called "genius" would be the
norm. The tremendous significance of Lenin's revolution
(*and* Douglas's economics) was that it promised to clear
"bread-and-butter problems" out of the way and
establish much more favourable conditions for this all-
important evolutionary process. "If Communism did not
mean *that* . . . if it only meant raising the economic level
of everybody until it was as high as that of the wealthiest
man in the world to-day, I would not move a little finger
to assist in the process."[26]

> Wanted a technique for genius! Or, at least,
> A means whereby a' genius yet has done
> 'll be the startin' point o' a' men's lives,
> No' zero, as if life had scarce begun,
> But to owrecome this death sae faur *ª*ben in
>   Maist folk needs the full floo'er o' Lenin.

> Be this the measure o' oor will to bring
> Like cruelty to a' men—nocht else'll dae;
> The source o' inspiration drooned in bluid
> If need be, owre and owre, until its ray
> Strengthens in a' forever or's hailly gane
>   As noo save in an *ᵇ*antrin brain.[27]

>   *ª* within   *ᵇ* occasional, rare

The "cruelty" that has to be brought to all men is the
suffering of genius, the necessary concomitant of any step
upwards on the evolutionary ladder since Man has become aware (however dimly and partially) of the ladder
itself. And on the political level the cruelty is that of "the
Cheka's horrors," amorally justified on the theory that
the end justifies the means, since revolution is seen as a
way of speeding up the evolution of mankind.

> *Oh, it's nonsense, nonsense, nonsense,*
> *Nonsense at this time o' day*
> *That breid-and-butter problems*
> *S'ud be in ony man's way.*

> *They s'ud be like the tails we ªtint*   *ª lost*
> *On leavin' the monkey stage;*
> *A' maist folk ᵇfash aboot's alike*   *ᵇ fuss*
> *Primæval to oor age.*[28]

The rightness or wrongness of MacDiarmid's political position is not at issue here. In any case, it would be something of a miracle if a man who despised mere logical consistency in every other respect were to be a party-liner in his politics; and in point of fact he interpreted Communist doctrine in his own highly individualist way. What is important here is to get the political element into perspective with regard to the poems he was writing at the time. The politics showed up more conspicuously because his position was becoming more definitely revolutionary: but his principal theme was the mystery of *epopteia*, the source of genius, the enlargement of consciousness.

In returning imaginatively to "The Muckle Toon," MacDiarmid was probing the source of his own inspiration and, more plainly (since he has never been in any doubt about it), his own genius. The imagery of these poems is drawn largely from boyhood memories of places and people, particularly his relatives, and it sometimes happens that light is shed on the poems by the little-known Scots prose pieces which he had contributed to periodicals some years before (1927–8). The prose and poetry mutually confirm how strong the autobiographical element was in his work at the time.

The dominant symbolism is of water, since "a perfect maze of waters is aboot the Muckle Toon," and in following the streams of his boyhood to their source, he passes from the mystery of genius to the origin and evolution of life itself:

> *And aye the force that's brocht life up*
> *Frae chaos to the present stage*
> *Creates new states as ill for us*
> *As oors for eels to gauge.*[29]

One begins to realise how that characteristic sense of the newly created world which is imprinted on so many of his poems comes from the actual experience of his childhood. The rivers Wauchope, Esk, and Ewes are now set free from the artificialities of the "Water of Life" in *Northern Numbers* and return through the poem of the same name and "Excelsior" in the *First Hymn* to their rhythmical apotheosis in the "Water Music" of *Scots Unbound*:

Lively, *a*louch, atweesh, atween,	*a* downcast
*b*Auchimuty or aspate,	*b* mean, thin
Threidin' through the *c*averins	*c* cloud-berries
Or *d*bightsom in the aftergait.[30]	*d* running easily

"The promise that there'll be nae second Flood" he takes "wi a' the salt I've saved since then," linking the fierce religion of his ancestors with those wonderful Waterside folk who are celebrated in the finest of the Scots prose sketches, "The Waterside," and again in the poem called "Excelsior":

Their queer stane faces and hoo green they got!
Juist like Rebecca in her shawl o' sly.
I'd never faur to gang to see doon there
A wreathéd Triton blaw his horn or try,
While at his feet a clump o' mimulus shone
    Like a dog's een wi' a' the world a bone.[31]

Norman McCaig has shrewdly remarked that the words "or try" in the fourth line of the above quotation could only have been written by MacDiarmid. They bear his signature. So does the last line of the following:

Spring to the North has aye come slow
But noo dour winter's like to stay
    For guid,
    And no' for guid![32]

What these two very different examples have in common is a "literal" feeling for words that is peculiar to Mac-

Diarmid, though there is something akin to it in James Joyce. It is a special aspect of the insatiable interest in words as such which, in combination with vast powers of memory, enables MacDiarmid to devour dictionaries and construct verbal *tours de force* like "Scots Unbound," "Tarras," "Water Music," "Balefire Loch," and parts of "Depth and the Chthonian Image." The first of these is subtitled "*Divertissement philologique*," and that is essentially what it is, although it may be noted how the river Esk slips into the picture (as into so many of the poems of this period) and turns his thoughts back to his Muse once again. The reader has to do his homework with Jamieson and others at his elbow before he is in a position to appreciate this "exercise of delight in the Scots sense of colour"[33] and, to a lesser extent, smell and taste. It is an "exercise" for the reader, too—a kind of verbal gymnastics, not relished by everybody.

"Water Music" is in a different category, not because its vocabulary is easier in itself, but because it is rhythmically such a delight that the literal meaning is an added satisfaction rather than a necessary condition of enjoyment. One reads first of all by ear, looks up the meaning of the words one has not been able to guess or "feel," and then returns to take even greater pleasure from the rhythm. In its original form, the poem is in two parts— the second not matching the sheer brilliance of the first, and therefore omitted by MacDiarmid from his *Selected* but not *Collected Poems*—beginning and ending with the injunction to James Joyce:

> *Wheesht, wheesht, Joyce, and let me hear*
> *Nae Anna Livvy's lilt,*
> *But Wauchope, Esk, and Ewes again,*
> *Each wi' its ain rhythms [a]till't.*[34]　　　[a] to it

It is a brave man who invites comparison with the author of *Anna Livia Plurabelle* in the handling of rhythm. MacDiarmid carries it off magnificently.

It is necessary to underline once more the poet's splendid ear for rhythm because of what will be said later about his subsequent development. Though sometimes marred by carelessness, his sense of rhythm was of the very first order, and as late as 1932 it can be seen at its finest in "Milk-wort and Bog-cotton," well known as one of his most perfect lyrics. Less well known is "The Hole in the Wall," which appeared in the *First Hymn* collection of the previous year, and which offers the following illustration of his rhythmical sense—and, at the beginning, his carelessness about such things as inversion. The poet is talking to one of his Langholm relatives:

As in mony a poem the emphasis
O' the poet's expression we ᵃtine   ᵃ lose
Through no' understandin' the metrical structure
Sae wi' lives like yours and mine.

Like when Uncle Dick wi' his ᵃpinkie crookt   ᵃ little
     Made yon gesture o' his,   finger
A raither slow line, half-blocked, half-reprovin'
     And suddenly Liz
     —Dirty Dick! Liz-Quiz!—
In a slightly buoyant anapaestic tone
     Threw the dog a bone,
And a wealth o' new rhythms was syne let loose
To mither's dismay, a' through the hoose.[35]

The aural qualities of language are naturally of great importance in those poems that employ a very unfamiliar vocabulary of dictionary Scots. The ear has to bridge *lacunae* in the sense, and, in particular, the rhythm must keep the strange words from clogging and clotting when they are used very thickly; otherwise the reader may be oppressed by a sense of mere verbalism. "Tarras" is a great *tour de force* in this respect—a celebration of "the auld vulture" of the bog, the earth-mother and bed-mate of "the hairy ones," that again will stand comparison with the Joyce of *Finnegans Wake*, though of course there is a fundamental difference in the linguistic techniques involved.

Some measure of MacDiarmid's range may be indicated by the fact that he was also using Scots for radically different purposes: firstly in the two "Hymns," which are not in any sense eulogies but rather man-to-man estimates of the importance of Lenin's achievement— Lenin as the new type of the modern hero, not at all a romantic "personality" as of old—and secondly in the "Ex-Parte Statement on the Project of Cancer," which makes science a spring-board for imaginative speculation. Finally, if there is such a thing as a "proletarian poetry" for our time, fit to be compared with the best popular poetry of the past, it is to be found in "The Seamless Garment," where the poet explains to a Langholm mill-worker the significance of Lenin and Rilke in terms of weaver and machine and of the proverbial wisdom of the housewife, ending shrewdly by adopting the weaver's test of good cloth for his own poetry. There is no condescension in all this. It is straight man-to-man stuff, in which the limitation of colloquial Scots—the fact that it is now largely confined to the usage of under-educated working folk—is seen to have its own virtue:

> Are you equal to life as to the loom?
>   Turnin' oot shoddy or what?
> Claith better than man? D'ye live to the full,
>   Your poo'ers a' *a*deliverly taught?   *a* consistently
> Or scamp a'thing else? Border claith's famous,
> Shall things o' mair consequence shame us?[36]

In *Stony Limits* (1934) there are relatively few poems in Scots, and only "Balefire Loch" gets the full synthetic treatment, while all but the title-poem of *Second Hymn to Lenin and Other Poems* (1935) are in English. One of the reasons behind this change is suggested in "Towards a New Scotland":

... My dreams for you, Scotland, as soon as I heard
Ithers cry I was richt and repeat what I'd said
I kent I was hopelessly wrang and was glad
O' the licht sic fools inadvertently shed![37]

One may suspect that there were other reasons as well.
But before considering why MacDiarmid kicked the synthetic Scots ladder away at this point, there are two
other matters which should be given some attention.

REFERENCES

1. *F.G.S.*, p. 42.
2. *C.C.*, pp. 20–1 (153–4).
3. *A.S.T.*, pp. 30–2.
4. *C.C.*, pp. 81, 103 (177, 186).
5. *C.C.*, p. 77.
6. *C.C.*, p. 64.
7. *C.C.*, p. 65.
8. *C.C.*, p. 97 (183).
9. *C.C.*, p. 107 (188).
10. *C.C.*, p. 15, 121.
11. *C.C.*, p. 101 (185).
12. *C.C.*, p. 112.
13. *C.C.*, p. 138.
14. *Alb.*, pp. 6–7.
15. *C.C.*, p. 82 (177). (Mac-Mhaighstir is Alexander MacDonald, by common consent the greatest of the Scots Gaelic poets.)
16. *The Present Condition of Scottish Arts and Affairs*, p. 7. Probable date is 1927, though MacDiarmid has suggested 1926.
17. See *L.P.*, p. 5.
18. *C.C.*, p. 52 (167). *Gaelic Literature Surveyed*, p. 52.
19. *Alb.*, p. 11.
20. *C.C.*, p. 88.
21. *Magnus Merriman*, London 1934, p. 105.
22. *C.C.*, p. 185.
23. For details of *Clann Albann* see *M.S.*, July. 1931, p. 107; and *S.O.*, 12 Aug. 1933, p. 10.
24. *S.O.*, 12 Aug. 1933, p. 10.
25. *S.O.*, 27 Jan. 1933, p. 11.
26. *L.P.*, p. 237.
27. "The Burning Passion," in *1st H.*, p. 23.
28. *2nd H.*, p. 7 (300).
29. "Excelsior," in *1st H.*, p. 42 (296).
30. *S.U.*, p. 5 (270).
31. *1st H.*, p. 44 (297).
32. *C.C.*, p. 44 (165).
33. *S.L.*, p. 109.
34. *S.U.*, p. 5 (270).
35. *1st H.*, p. 30.
36. *1st H.*, p. 35 (291).
37. *S.L.*, p. 102 (233).

CHAPTER V

VERSE TRANSLATIONS AND SCOTS PROSE

One of the surprises in MacDiarmid's work in Scots was the inclusion of poems and passages translated or adapted from modern German, Russian, French and Belgian poets. Particularly in *A Drunk Man*, he tended to take suggestions from these writers, or adapt their poems to his own purposes, rather than give straight translations.

The untitled poem "suggested by the German of Else Lasker-Schüler"[1] is a particularly interesting example of this. The title of the German original is *Sphynx*, and the whole thing is built round the image of the sphinx, but MacDiarmid's lines are made to refer to the moon, which is of course one of his key-symbols in *A Drunk Man*. This is not so great a change as might be supposed; the sphinx does in fact become "die Mondfrau" at the end of Else Lasker-Schüler's poem.[2] However, MacDiarmid follows her only for the first five lines. He then jumps to the end of her poem, focuses on the phrase "Kampf mit Widerspruechen," and introduces another of his own key-symbols, the thistle, to embody this "struggle with contradictions." Completely jettisoned in the process is the flowery boudoir imagery of Else Lasker-Schüler's second stanza, which gives her poem its characteristic "black swan of Israel" atmosphere. The transformation is radical:

Sphynx

Sie sitzt an meinem Bette in der Abendzeit
Une meine Seele tut nach ihrem Willen,
Und in der Daemmerscheine, traumestillen

Engen wie Faeden duenn sich ihre Glanzpupillen
Um ihrer Sinne schlaefrige Geschmeidigkeit.

Und auf dem Nebenbette an den Leinennaehten
Knistern die Spitzenranken von Narzissen,
Und ihre Haende dehnen breit sich nach dem Kissen,
Auf dem noch Traueme bluchn aus seinen Kuessen,
Herzsuesser Duft auf weissen Beeten.

Und laechelnd taucht die Mondfrau in die
        Wolkenwellen
Und meine bleichen, leidenden Psychen
Erstarken neu im Kampf mit Widerspruechen.

The Mune sits on my bed the nicht unsocht,
And mak's my soul obedient to her will;
And in the dumb-deid, still as dreams are still,
Her pupils narraw to bricht threids that thrill
Aboot the sensuous windin's o' her thocht.

But ilka windin' has its coonter-pairt
—The opposite 'thoot which it couldna be—
In some wild kink or queer perversity
O' this great thistle, green wi' jealousy,
That ᵃbreenges 'twixt the munelicht and my hert.   ᵃ plunges

One is certainly impressed by the mysterious instinct
which led MacDiarmid to remember what could be of
use to him in a poem that would otherwise seem so foreign
to his purposes in *A Drunk Man*. However, by specifying
the language of the original—"suggested by the *German*"
—he invited his readers to conclude that he was working
directly from it. If so, the following version of the first
stanza by Babette Deutsch and Avrahm Yarmolinsky
presents some remarkable coincidences:

She sits upon my bed at dusk, unsought,
And makes my soul obedient to her will,
And in the twilight, still as dreams are still,

> Her pupils narrow to bright threads that thrill
> About the sensuous windings of her thought.

Elsewhere in MacDiarmid's first three volumes of verse there are poems, adapted or otherwise, from the *Russian* of Alexander Blok, Zinaida Hippius, and Dmitry Merezhkovsky; the *German* of Stefan George and Rudolf Leonhardt; the *French* of Edmond Rocher and Gustave Kahn. Why should he repeatedly specify the language, if not to suggest that he was working directly from it? Yet every one of these poems may be found in English versions by Deutsch and Yarmolinsky or Jethro Bithell which were published before MacDiarmid's Scots ones appeared.[3]

Not to put too fine a point on it, the reader may compare the following three versions of a sample from Alexander Blok, and draw his own conclusions:

> And every evening, strange, immutable,
> (Is it a dream no waking proves?)
> As to a rendezvous inscrutable
> A silken lady darkly moves.
> > [DEUTSCH and YARMOLINSKY][4]

> *But ilka evenin' fey and fremt*
> *(Is it a dream nae wauk'nin' proves?)*
> *As to a trystin'-place undreamt,*
> *A silken leddy darkly moves.*
> > [MACDIARMID][5]

> Each evening at the hour concerted
> > To misty window there draws nigh
> A maiden's form, in silk gown skirted—
> > Or is this but my dreaming eye?
> > > [KISCH][6]

MacDiarmid's Scots versions have sufficient genuine accomplishment to dispense with equivocations about how they came to be written, so why beat about the bush

where his knowledge of foreign languages is concerned?
There can be no doubt that he has a remarkable facility
in picking up a working knowledge of diverse languages,
but there is no convincing evidence to show that he is in
full command of any foreign tongue. The specimen of
his own French verse in *Sangschaw*, "La Fourmilière,"
leaves much to be desired.

Not that MacDiarmid has made active efforts to cover
his tracks where his translations or adaptations are concerned. He himself mentions the fact that "Bithell's little
volumes" were his introduction to many modern German
poets.[7] And one is amused by the line addressed to
Dostoevsky—"I ken nae Russian and you ken nae
Scots"—in a section of the *Drunk Man* where the terms
narodbogonosets and *vse-chelovek* have previously been used.
But it is as well to try to clarify what comes from the
hoaxing side of MacDiarmid and what does not, since
otherwise a serious-minded reader is liable to take offence
and miss the poet's real achievement.

What he does with his materials, whatever their source,
is well worth attention. A poem like the Belgian Georges
Ramaekers' "Thistle," which comes over effectively in
Bithell's English translation, and which is so obviously
appropriate to MacDiarmid's *Drunk Man* theme, is put
into Scots straightforwardly, with only an occasional
modification of the sense.[8] Zinaida Hippius's "Psyche,"
Englished by Deutsch and Yarmolinsky, is reworked
more thoroughly, and the concluding lines are changed
brilliantly so as to link Hippius's image of the octopus
with Melville's white whale, and thus stretch its associations on the wider framework of *A Drunk Man*:

> And this dead thing, this loathesome black impurity,
> This horror that I shrink from—is my soul.[9]

> *And this deid thing, whale-white obscenity,*
> *This horror that I writhe in—is my soul.*[10]

The serpent from Ramaekers and the dragon from Hippius are similarly absorbed into the rich context of MacDiarmid's poem; from Blok he takes over the most appropriate themes of strong drink and mysterious woman, subtly remodelling many of the lines in the process; and from Edmond Rocher he takes the merest hint from the last two lines of a poem in *Le Manteau du passé* and works it up into one of his most powerful and most characteristic statements of what underlies the sexual relationship.

Bithell had translated some poems by Rilke as early as 1909, but not the "Requiem für eine Freundin," an English adaptation of which MacDiarmid included in *Cencrastus*. He cut away more than a quarter of the original, and transposed and altered a passage so as to have his adaptation end on a much stronger note than does Rilke's poem:

> Even as a landsman's eyesight fails to hold
> The Deity on the shoulders of a ship,
> When its own lightness lifts it suddenly
> Up and away into the bright sea wind. . . .[11]

In Rilke, this image occurs about fifty lines before the end. A faithful rendering by J. B. Leishman runs as follows:

> As little as the captain can retain
> the niké poised upon his vessel's prow
> when the mysterious lightness of her godhead
> has caught her up into the limpid sea-wind.[12]

There are a number of other interesting changes, apart from the cutting and compressing, but one brief example will have to suffice here. Rilke's actual words are followed by Leishman's more or less literal translation and then by MacDiarmid's version:

> Lass uns zusammen klagen dass dich einer
> aus deinem Spiegel nahm.[13]

Let both of us lament that someone took you
out of your mirror.[14]

Let us lament together—the broken mirror
And you found naked in your hiding place.[15]

The great virtue of MacDiarmid's adaptation is that it
sounds more like an original poem in English than a
translation, and it is so finely written, particularly with
regard to rhythm, that it makes one feel that Rilke's
poem *must* be a fine one.

As to the English verse translation of Gaelic poems
which MacDiarmid made with the help of Sorley
MacLean, there is general agreement amongst compe-
tent judges that they are among the best extant.[16] This
may not be saying very much. However, as Eliot remarked of Chinese poetry and Ezra Pound, Scots Gaelic
poetry as many people know it to-day is something
invented by MacDiarmid.

MacDiarmid's prose in Scots is virtually unknown,
except for two dramatised sketches which were included
in *Scottish Scene* (1934). Both of these—"Some Day" and
"The Purple Patch"—are early pieces, dating from 1923
and 1924 respectively,[17] and they do not reveal much
talent for drama in their author. So far as performance in
a theatre is concerned, "The Purple Patch" would present
formidable problems, as members of three different groups
of characters are required to make long speeches *simultaneously*. This idea came from a lecture on music by
Walford Davies in which he invited his audience to
imagine "a little play in which three people spoke all the
time, always speaking independent things, but managing
to be inter-dependent." MacDiarmid conceded that his
"Cross-Talk Comedy in One Act" was probably not
actable—"but the Scottish National Players should
make sure." He also drew the attention of local drama
groups to three other plays he had written by May 1924,
"all alike experimental—each in a different direction."

One of them was "an actionless drama of a new type—a
sort of *liaison* between the monologue and that most
difficult form of literary art, the epistolary novel."[18]

His non-dramatised prose pieces in Scots are not experimental, and some of them are of no technical interest
at all. When he adopts a *persona* here it is generally that
of a more or less simple-minded, under-educated, rusti-
cated character, in keeping with the subject-matter,
which is worked up from local lore and legend. Otherwise the author speaks with the voice of his own boyhood,
and again there is a simplification of attitude, a restric-
tion of range that is reflected in the formal treatment and
in the texture of the language, which is usually a rather
thin, colloquial Scots—accurately recorded but not
deployed with any great distinction. There is little
heightening or intensifying of the local tongue, not even
rhythmically—a great loss in MacDiarmid. The medium
of expression is basically the same as that used in the
dramatised sketches, which is naturally very close to
actual dialect speech—though "The Purple Patch" does
take a few lines of verse from Jamieson and put them in
the mouth of old Mrs Roebuck, a lady "far gone in
senile decay."

"A' Body's Lassie" has more in common with folk
tales, set in the country towns of his youth, than with
literature as such; and the longest of these pieces,
"Murtholm Hill," is technically no more ambitious,
leaving one with the impression of a writer who is compe-
tent enough in his simple way but not specially gifted. So
also with the macabre, or the humorous treatment of the
supernatural, in stories such as "A Dish o' Whummle" or
"The Visitor": the technical resources are too simple to
stimulate one's interest, and the language is too little
manipulated, too much of a mere recording.

One of these stories appeared in the *Scots Magazine*; the
others (along with "Holie for Nags," a memory of boyhood) in the *Scots Observer* (1927–8). But the best of the

prose pieces appeared in the *Glasgow Herald* (1927):
"Andy," "Maria," "The Common Riding"—spoiled,
however, by an excess of sentimental patriotism at the
end—"The Moon Through Glass," and "The Waterside."[19]

The material of the *Glasgow Herald* stories again comes
from memories of MacDiarmid's childhood in or around
Langholm, or, in the case of "The Moon Through
Glass," from traditional, popular superstition. But the
sense of form is sharper, and the language is handled with
much greater skill. More of the artist in MacDiarmid is
allowed to come into play, for all that the language is
faithful to dialect speech, and there is a corresponding
gain in psychological perception and precise observation.

The highwater mark is reached in more senses than
one by "The Waterside," which MacDiarmid ought to
put into a book along with "The Moon Through Glass,"
two or three of the other Scots pieces, "Five-Bits of
Miller," "The Scab," and as many other pieces in
English as he can find to approach that standard. Full of
dry humour, shrewd psychology, a dead-pan treatment
of the macabre, and sudden, unexpected touches of fan-
tasy, "The Waterside" is marred only by MacDiarmid's
cavalier attitude towards such incidentals as the ortho-
graphy of Scots. It is also a splendid complement to
several of his poems:

The waterside folk kept [a]skitin' this way and that.
There was neither peace nor profit in their lives. They
couldna settle. Their kind of life was like the dipper's
sang. It needit the [b]skelp and slither o' runnin' water
like the bagpipes' drone to fill oot the blanks. Withoot
that it was naething but a [c]spraichle o' jerky and
meaningless soonds. . . .

It was only in the winter time that the water exer-
cised its poo'er owre the haill toon. The hills were
hidden in mists then and the folk that were aye

accustomed to them were at a loss. They were like a
[d]puckle water when a jug braks: they'd [e]tint the shape
o' their lives. . . .

The Waterside folk lived in their doors or windas as
gin their hooses had nae insides. They could do naething but look, or raither be lookit at, through and
through, for it was the water that did the lookin' and
no' them. There was nae question o' thinkin'. It was
faur owre quick and noisy for that. It fair [f]deaved
them, and every noo and then a muckle wave loupit in
through their een and swirled in their [g]toom harnpans
and oot again. That's what I mean when I say that the
Waterside folk were brainless craturs. Brains were nae
use there. To dae onything [h]ava they'd to use something faur quicker than thocht—something as auld as
water itsel'. And thocht's a dryland thing and a [i]gey
recent [j]yin at that.[20]

| [a] flying off | [b] slap | [c] scramble | [d] little | [e] lost |
| [f] stunned | [g] empty skulls | [h] at all | [i] very | [j] one |

REFERENCES

1. *D.M.*, pp. 15–16 (76–7).
2. "Sphynx," in *Gedichte, 1902–1943*, Munchen 1959, p. 148.
3. *Contemporary Belgian Poetry*, London 1911. *Contemporary French Poetry*, London 1912. *Contemporary German Poetry*, London 1923. *Modern Russian Poetry*, London 1923.
4. *Modern Russian Poetry*, p. 129.
5. *D.M.*, p. 8 (69).
6. Sir Cecil Kisch, *Alexander Blok: Prophet of Revolution*, London 1960, p. 43.
7. *L.P.*, pp. 82–3.
8. *D.M.*, p. 78 (73).
9. *Modern Russian Poetry*, p. 70.
10. *D.M.*, p. 14 (77).
11. *C.C.*, p. 41 (163).
12. J. B. Leishman (trans.), *Rainer Maria Rilke—Requiem and Other Poems*, London, 1949, p. 135.
13. Rainer Maria Rilke, *Sämtliche Werks*, Insel-Verlag 1955, I, p. 650.
14. J. B. Leishman, *op. cit.*, p. 132.
15. *C.C.*, p. 36 (161).
16. See in particular the translations of Alexander MacDonald and Duncan Ban

MacIntyre in *G.T.*, pp. 43–58, 65–85.

17. "Some Day," in *S.N.*, 30 Oct. 1923, pp. 10–11. "The Purple Patch," in *N.R.*, May 1924, pp. 16–21.

18. "Causerie," in *N.R.*, May 1924, p. 2. The titles of the plays are *Jenny Spells*, *The Candidate*, and *The Morning Post*.

19. See *G.H.*, 12 Mar., 16 Apr., 16 Jul., 27 Aug. 1927. *S.O.*, 19 Mar., 14 May, 1 Oct. 1927; 22 Sep. 1928. *S.M.*, Apr. 1927, pp. 1–11.

"A Dish of Whummle" appeared as "Wound-Pie" [*sic*] along with "A'Body's Lassie" and two English stories by MacDiarmid in *New Tales of Horror*, London [*c.* 1934]. It was altered by the editor to accord with his misunderstanding of the Scots *wund* (=wind). "The Moon Through Glass" appeared in *Path and Pavement* (ed. John Rowland), London 1937.

20. *G.H.*, 16 Apr. 1927, p. 4.

CHAPTER VI

SYNTHETIC ENGLISH, SCIENCE, AND PROPAGANDA

When the *Stony Limits* collection appeared in 1934, it confirmed a tendency already evident in MacDiarmid's recent contributions to periodicals whereby he had been writing his poems alternately in a thin variety of Scots or in southern English, with a growing preference for the latter. In the following year, only the title-poem of a collection of nearly fifty in the *Second Hymn* volume was in Scots, and it had definitely been written at least three years before. Since then, he has written almost entirely in English.

The picture is clear, a little too clear. For in MacDiarmid's periodical *The Voice of Scotland* for September and December 1947, eight poems from the *Second Hymn* volume figured as parts of a long "Ode to All Rebels,"[1] and six of these were then in *Scots*. Furthermore, internal evidence showed that the Scots versions must have preceded the English ones, which suggested in turn that the "Ode" might have been written prior to 1935. That this was in fact the case was confirmed by MacDiarmid only in 1956, when he revealed that his publishers had deleted the complete poem from the manuscript of *Stony Limits*.[2]

The "Ode to All Rebels" is the longest *sustained* flight (about 800 lines) that MacDiarmid has achieved since the *Drunk Man*, which it resembles in some respects, especially in the opening sections, where sex is the dominant theme. This, along with some passages that might be regarded as blasphemous by a nervous lawyer, is presumably the reason why his publisher rejected it. The simple colloquial Scots in which most of it is written would be much

easier for the censorial mind to grasp than the language
of the *Drunk Man*. The same is true of the still more
dangerous *Harry Semen*, deleted from the same manuscript, though it appeared in the *Modern Scot*[3] in 1933 and
in the *Selected Poems* of 1944. Both poems are written in a
strong, forceful style, and, had they appeared as planned
in *Stony Limits*, they would have forestalled some at least
of the critical confusion regarding MacDiarmid's transition from Scots to English as his principal linguistic
medium.

In particular, the "Ode" shows that MacDiarmid at
that time was able to recover a good part of the ground
lost by *Cencrastus* in his "gallimaufry" form of thought-
narrative interspersed with lyrics. The linguistic medium
is more or less the same as that of *Cencrastus*, but the
quality of the poetry is not far from the very high average
of the *Drunk Man*:

> Cataclysm in the mirror. What's that I see?
> I heard reason shriek and saw her flee
> Through the [a]weiks o' my e'e   [a] corners
> And kent it was me.[4]

At the same time, the drift towards "standard" English—
the cause of much angry frustration in *Cencrastus*—is no
longer resisted. The final section of the "Ode" draws to
an impressive conclusion in the southern language:

> Your song, O God, that none dare hear
> Save the insane and such as I
> Apostates from humanity
> Sings out in me with no more fear
> Than one who thinks he has the world's ear
> From his padded cell
> —Insane enough, with you so near,
> To want, like you, the world as well.[5]

The question of which language to use does not appear
to be a problem of special importance, and one certainly

does not feel that MacDiarmid is "abandoning" Scots for specifically linguistic reasons. Rather, he seems to gravitate into English in a perfectly natural way, obeying some inner instinct which tells him that he can no longer "follow up the *Drunk Man* line." Much later, he was to say that this situation was brought about by crises in his personal life.[6]

Apparently there was a partial blockage of the emotional springs that had sustained the lyric intensity and exhilaration of the *Drunk Man*. At any rate the turning to English accompanied an approach to poetry in which the element of *lyrical* inspiration was no longer relied upon to anything like the same extent.

The *Clann Albann* project was put aside, and so also was the plan for a "companion volume" to *A Drunk Man* called *The Frontier: Or the War with England*, which seems in any case to have been a very shaky affair.[7] MacDiarmid became particularly interested in the possibilities of science for poetry—largely non-lyrical possibilities, of course—and after a few experiments in mixing scientific terminology with his synthetic Scots, he concentrated on using that terminology within the context of standard English. This was a logical move, since the intensive employment of a specialised scientific diction in English verse was quite novel, and involved a sufficient number of problems in itself, without the added complication of importing all the scientific terms into Scots. Considered as a distinct national language, Scots had ceased to develop before modern science got under way, and had little or nothing of its own to offer even to the terminology of the industrial revolution.

The procedure of simply giving English scientific terms a Scottish accent was not of much account to MacDiarmid—though there might be certain advantages to it if one wished like Wordsworth to domesticate science. On the other hand, if, as MacDiarmid had said more than thirty years before, "the problem is to determine what 'motor-car' would have been in the Doric had the Doric ... become an all-sufficient independent language," he no longer believed that such problems, multiplied over and over again, could be solved by him or even by his generation:

> We have an enormous leeway to make up. I think the resources of Scots are adequate to the purpose; I think we can apply them. But it is not a job that can be done by one man or perhaps even in one lifetime. It may take several generations of intensive work along that line.[8]

In the meanwhile, MacDiarmid applied himself to the existing scientific terminology of English as offering a possibility of fresh linguistic sustenance that the English poets themselves had barely begun to be aware of. But his lexicophagus habits soon took him beyond the more obvious fields of science to "recondite elements of the English vocabulary"[9] wherever these were to be found; and out of all this came a "synthetic English" on which he began to draw for a new kind of poetic diction. A mild example is afforded by the closing lines of "In the Caledonian Forest," where his subject keeps him fairly close to the conventional sources of poetic imagery in Nature, and leads him to include a couple of Scots words in the amalgam:

> The gold edging of a bough at sunset, its pantile way
> Forming a double curve, tegula and imbrex in one,
> Seems at times a movement on which I might be
>   borne
> Happily to infinity; but again I am glad
> When it suddenly ceases and I find myself
> Pursuing no longer a rhythm of duramen
> But bouncing on the diploe in a clearing between
>   earth and air
> Or headlong in dewy dallops or a moon-spairged
>   fernshaw

Or caught in a dark dumosity or even
In open country again watching an aching spargosis
   of stars.[10]

More drastically, in some cases, the esoteric diction
insulates the poem from the familiar world of the senses and
the emotions—including most aesthetic emotions—the
words being placed like so many cryptic pieces on the
chess-board of the poet's mind. A very good dictionary
will supply names for the pieces, but not much more than
that. Only as they are moved in and out of the shifting
gambits of thought can they begin to exist in rhythmic
relationships—a rhythm that appeals more often to the
brain than to the ear. It is as though the poet has to put
connotations into the words, instead of the usual procedure of drawing them out. And once the initial novelty
has worn off, the game becomes excessively tiring.

MacDiarmid did not play it very often, however. His
method with experimental techniques is to push them
immediately to the extreme, as if to see how much they
can stand. And in this particular instance the breaking-
point was quickly reached. When everything is more or
less equally unfamiliar, there is nothing left for the unfamiliarity to refer back to. And especially where the
terminology of the sciences is concerned, it should be
remembered that MacDiarmid had just thrown an
Anarchist "Ode" in the teeth of

A' the men o' science, the enemies o' truth . . .
A' that expect clear explanations,
Fixed standards and reasonable methods.[11]

As a matter of fact, one of the most interesting of the
Stony Limits poems uses the terminology of science to
attack scientific rationalism. MacDiarmid had said, back
in 1923, that he was "quite certain that the imagination
had some way of dealing with the truth which the reason
had not, and that commandments delivered when the

body is still and the reason silent are the most binding
that the souls of men can ever know."[12] Now, in the poem
"Thalamus," he translated this perception into terms of
the anatomy of the brain, saying that it was from the
"older, darker, less studied regions of cranial anatomy"
that there came

> The truths that all great thinkers have seen
> At the height of their genius—and then
> Spent most of their days denying
> Or trying to scale down to mere reason's ken
> —The height to which all life must tend
> And securely hold at the end.
>
> But proud of their cortex few
> Have glimpsed the medial nuclei yet
> Of their thalamus—that Everest in themselves
> Reason should have explored before it
> As the corpora geniculata before any star
> To know what and why men are.[13]

To write in such a way you need more than a dictionary of science. You have to make information supplied by
science part of the process of imaginative thought. And
this is what MacDiarmid does in the best of these poems.
He may begin with limbering-up exercises for the brain,
or pelt it with exotic vocables so that it goes running back
and forth between the dictionary and the poem, ferrying
meanings: but then he will settle down to his line of
thought, and it is well worth following him. Thus he
begins "On a Raised Beach":

> All is lithogenesis—or lochia,
> Carpolite fruit of the forbidden tree,
> Stones blacker than any in the Caaba,
> Cream-coloured caen-stone, chatoyant pieces,
> Celadon and corbeau, bistre and beige,
> Glaucous, hoar, enfouldered, cyathiform,
> Making mere faculae of the sun and moon . . .[14]

—and so on for another ten lines before we get, not a
period, of course, but a question mark. Then between the
clear light and the pure water of the treeless Shetlands a
single bird moves among the stones, and the stones are
seen as never before:

> There are plenty of ruined buildings in the world
> > but no ruined stones. . . .
>
> This is no heap of broken images. . . .
>
> These stones go through Man, straight to God, if
> > there is one.
> What have they not gone through already?
> Empires, civilisations, æons. Only in them
> If in anything, can His creation confront Him.
> They came so far out of the water and halted forever.
> That larking dallier, the sun, has only been able to
> > play
> With superficial by-products since;
> The moon moves the water backwards and forwards,
> But the stones cannot be lured an inch further
> Either on this side of eternity or the other.
> Who thinks God is easier to know than they are?[15]

The imaginative penetration into the world of stones
proceeds from a solid basis of geological knowledge. This
science had a special attraction for MacDiarmid, and
when he went to live in the Shetlands he spent much of
his time in the company of a geologist, exploring the little
islands around Whalsay. The vast solitude, the audible
silence, the sense of the skull beneath the skin of the
world, all told him that "there are no twirly bits in this
ground bass," and the impersonality of scientific fact
harmonised with bare landscape and seascape:

> > What happens to us
> > Is irrelevant to the world's geology
> > But what happens to the world's geology
> > Is not irrelevant to us.[16]

Light on water and rock, and "Los muertos abren los ojos a los que viven":

Perfect

I found a pigeon's skull on the machair,
All the bones pure white and dry, and chalky,
But perfect,
Without a crack or a flaw anywhere.

At the back, rising out of the beak,
Were twin domes like bubbles of thin bone,
Almost transparent, where the brain had been
That fixed the tilt of the wings.[17]

The above is the poem that Ezra Pound and the Imagists talked about but did not write, in which "the proper and perfect symbol is the natural object" itself.[18] It is also, in its second verse, an object lesson in the meaningful use of vowel-music, consonance, and alliteration. But it seems to have been intended as MacDiarmid's *Goodbye to All That*, already heralded in "The Point of Honour," where he had admonished himself:

No more of mere sound, the least part![19]

In this poem he visited in his imagination the Esk of his boyhood once again, confessed in humility to some mysterious lack in his inspiration, and ended as follows:

Already gleam
In the eyes of the young the flicker, the change,
The free enthusiasm that carries the stream
Suddenly out of my range.

Despite the occasion of the poem (subtitled "On Watching The Esk Again") he writes in English, not Scots, and allows himself the indulgence of imitating the technique of an old favourite of his, Gerald Manley Hopkins. The imitation is brilliant, but for MacDiarmid, with his declared intention only to do work that is *sui generis*, it indicates improvisation prior to setting off on a fresh tack.

G

Although MacDiarmid's mind has always been steeped in "a strong solution of books," it is only very rarely that one can point to a particular influence on the technique of a particular poem. The bare fact that F. R. Leavis[20] could refer specifically to D. H. Lawrence and the later Yeats with regard to certain pieces in the 1935 *Second Hymn* collection therefore reinforces the impression that this book is a gathering together of interim work. As was already indicated, some of the poems are Englished versions of parts of the "Ode to All Rebels." Others are linked to the "Ode" in the sense that they, too, say things in verse that we would expect to find—if at all—in a novel of the psychologically realistic variety. But it would be no ordinary novelist who could perceive with such merciless clarity, and state with such deep honesty, the psychological facts of "One of the Principal Causes of War" ("Jeannie MacQueen" in the Scots version) and "The Two Parents."

Neither "synthetic" nor even scientific English is present to any extent in this volume. However, "On the Ocean Floor" does make use of foraminifera *metaphorically,* and this indicates a more fruitful aspect of science for the poet: science as a source of fresh imagery. One of the best examples in MacDiarmid may be found as early as 1932:

Dytiscus

The problem in the pool is plain.
Must men to higher things ascend
For air like the Dytiscus there,
Breathe through their spiracles, and turn
To diving bells and seek their share
Of sustenance in the slime again
Till they clear life, as he his pool,
To starve in purity, the fool,
Their finished faculties mirrored, fegs,
Foiled-fierce as his three pairs of legs?
Praise be, Dytiscus-men are rare,

> Life's pool still foul and full of fare.
> Long till to suicidal success attain
> We water-beetles of the brain![21]

Several of the poems in the *Second Hymn* volume cast light on what had been the weakest part of *Stony Limits*, published in the previous year. Some show his fundamental attitude unchanged:

> On every thought I have the countless shadows fall
> Of other thoughts as valid that I cannot have;
> Cross-lights of errors, too, impossible to me,
> Yet somehow truer than all these thoughts, being
> with more power aglow. . . .
>
> I have not gained a single definite belief that can be
> put
> In a scientific formula or hardened into a religious
> creed. . . .
>
> But who from sperm to maturity
> Has come need have no fear
> To leave his further course to whatever
> Arranged that incredible career.[22]

But his poem on "The Covenanters" indicates the way the wind was blowing:

> The waves of their purposefulness go flooding
> through me.
> This religion is simple, naked. Its values stand out
> In black and white. . . .
> It holds me in a fastness of security.[23]

And "Poetry and Propaganda" ends as follows:

> In short, any utterance that is not pure
> Propaganda is impure propaganda for sure.[24]

Now it is arguable that all art is propaganda, but some specimens of this propaganda are better art than others.

And there are further distinctions that have to be made.
For example, it may be agreed that Coleridge's "Ancient
Mariner" is propaganda, but it is not propaganda on
behalf of a Society for the Prevention of Cruelty to
Albatrosses.

One's objection to some of the poems in *Stony Limits*
and the *Second Hymn* is not that they are propaganda as
such but rather that they are, firstly, badly-written
propaganda and, secondly, crude and oversimplified in
their message. They tell us only about Bad Guys and
Good Guys; their values "stand out in black and white"
precisely because they are crudely conceived; and they
do not utilise more than the barest fraction of the talents
of the man who wrote them.

Most of the propaganda is Douglasite, and one must
have every sympathy with the feelings of a man who,
living in conditions of extreme hardship for his family and
himself, and acutely aware of the economic miseries of
his country in the grim nineteen-thirties, yet believes
that for mankind

> The struggle for material existence is over. It has
> been won.[25]

But poems either good or bad may be written out of such
feelings, and poems such as "The Belly Grip" are bad
poems—and all the more so because they sometimes have
excellent lines in them, as is the case with "Genethliacon,"
for example.

MacDiarmid had written a fair amount of rough-and-
ready journalistic verse before *Stony Limits* appeared, but
never before had he put isolated specimens of it in a
collection of poetry along with work of a completely
different order of achievement. Why did he do so
now?

To answer that question one would have to be able to
explain why a poet who had always shown abundant
evidence of his wonderful ear for rhythm, and his instinct

for the word or phrase that would pull its full weight in the line of verse, should now offer this sort of thing:

> The fools who say men must still bear any yoke
> Have no gifts, save cruelty, more than most other
>   folk.[26]

How far is this the deliberate anti-poetry of a man who has turned his back on the "mere beauty" of the lyric (using "lyric" in the wide sense of the term)? And how far does it indicate a blunting of the sense of rhythm in the man himself, who, realising he has lost something, proceeds to undervalue it and, making a virtue of necessity, invests his capital elsewhere?

It would be idle to pretend that one can answer such questions with any real assurance. But one can at least point to a factor that has some bearing on the problems involved. MacDiarmid's experiments with "synthetic" and scientific English, using words that are often screened from our emotions, might be used in the building of what Denis Saurat called the Third Convention, "where men can think without first having to feel."[27] But where poetry is concerned, feeling is the touchstone of rhythm, and rhythm is connected with the sense of form. Thus, at the same time as MacDiarmid became interested in these experiments, one notes signs of uncertainty in his rhythm and ultimately in his form. Naturally, syntax was affected as well, especially in poems that retain rhyme but show little concern whether the rhyme exacts a heavy price by way of syntactical contortions, fill-up phrases, and mere tags like "I wis" (to rhyme with "is").

These are amongst the surface signs of a crisis in the man and the poet. His doctor, David Orr, has given an inkling into the disorientation which occurred in the summer of 1934, when MacDiarmid was also in poor condition physically, and which resulted in a spell in hospital. This illness was apparently due to "a summation of numerous subconscious 'insults' arising from domestic difficulties a few years previously."[28] He made a rapid recovery and was soon back in the Shetlands, but it is clear that the psychological need of the man for a fresh start had its effect on the poet's decision to employ a different sort of technical apparatus in his work. There is just a possibility also that an accident that occurred in London, back in December 1929, had some ultimate bearing on the poet's erratic handling of rhythm. He himself tells us, merely to introduce an excellent joke in *Lucky Poet*,[29] that on that occasion he fell from the top of a double-decker bus and landed on his head on the pavement. About three weeks in hospital with severe concussion followed.

Returning to less speculative ground, it was the apparatus rather than the aim of the poet that was to be changed. For many years he had seen possibilities for an epic poetry in the neglected Gaelic roots of Scotland, and his constant championship of Charles Doughty, to whom he addressed the noble elegy that supplied the title for *Stony Limits*, was mainly owing to Doughty's epic treatment of "the ancient British history"—that is, the history of *Celtic* Britain. This, and the fact that Doughty kept his eye firmly on East *and* West, is of much more fundamental importance to MacDiarmid than his predecessor's linguistic experiments, his "synthetic Anglo-Saxon." An impression to the contrary may have been given by MacDiarmid's habit of coupling Doughty's name with that of the great experimentalist Hopkins—these two being almost the only poets he thinks worthy of consideration in the history of English poetry "since Chaucer" (or, in his more generous moments, "since Shakespeare and Milton").[30] But the deeper significance lies in Doughty's having achieved at least partially, in the "heroic poetry" of *The Dawn in Britain*, what George Buchanan, Milton, Blake and Matthew Arnold had all contemplated but, for various reasons, failed to do.

The first specimen of MacDiarmid's own "heroic poetry" dealing with the ancient Celtic tradition, apparently abandoned but still capable of being repossessed in the spirit, is the long "Lament for the Great Music."[31] If all art is propaganda, this is propaganda for a return to the values of a civilisation in which the technical accomplishment of poetry or of *Ceol Mor*, the great classical music of the Highland bagpipe, was respected as part of the people's heritage. As far as his own technique was concerned, MacDiarmid now abandoned traditional metre and rhyme, and allowed himself very great freedom as to rhythm. His tendency to drop into prosaic kinds of rhythm—prosaic in the sense that our ear tells us they belong to prose contexts of a comparatively unimaginative order—is thus to some extent cushioned. But, freed from traditional disciplines, MacDiarmid lets the poem run on for too long. This is a great pity, as it contains some very fine, and deeply moving, passages.

Most of MacDiarmid's poems are self-centred, and this is not one of the exceptions, but the heroic level of the "Lament" is sustained by his sense of the greatness of the lost bardic tradition and the immense difficulty of the task he is setting himself in trying to bring it back to imaginative life:

> My native land should be to me
> As a root to a tree. If a man's labour fills no want there
> His deeds are doomed and his music mute. . . .
> But I am companioned by an irrecoverable past,
> By a mystical sense of such destiny foregone . . .
> Time out of mind.[32]

REFERENCES

1. Reprinted in *S.L.S.U.*, pp. 91–108.
2. "Author's Note," *S.L.S.U.*, p. v.
3. *M.S.*, Oct. 1933, pp. 185–7.
4. *S.L.S.U.*, p. 110.
5. *S.L.S.U.*, p. 118.
6. *D.M.*, 2nd edn., p. x.
7. See, *e.g.*, *F.M.*, 31 Mar. 1934, p. 7.
8. "Aims and Opinions," 9 Mar. 1960.
9. *S.L.S.U.*, p. v.
10. *S.L.S.U.*, p. 9.
11. *S.L.S.U.*, pp. 113–14.
12. *A.*, p. 189.
13. *S.L.S.U.*, p. 32.
14. *S.L.S.U.*, pp. 42–3.
15. *S.L.S.U.*, pp. 46, 48, 49.
16. *S.L.S.U.*, p. 50.
17. *S.P.*, p. 55 (322).
18. *Literary Essays of Ezra Pound*, London 1954, p. 9.
19. *S.L.S.U.*, p. 18 (206).
20. *Scrutiny*, Dec. 1935, p. 305.
21. *S.U.*, p. 30 (277).
22. *2nd H. & O.*, pp. 33, 73 (318–19), 66 (316).
23. *2nd H. & O.*, p. 51.
24. *2nd H. & O.*, p. 65.
25. *S.L.S.U.*, p. 143 (263).
26. *S.L.S.U.*, p. 12.
27. *C.C.*, p. 30.
28. "MacDiarmid—The Man," in *Jabberwock*, VOL. V, 1958, p. 15.
29. *L.P.*, p. 38.
30. Cp., *e.g.*, "Aims and Opinions" (1st Broadcast), 4 Mar. 1940, and *A.S.T.*, pp. 106–7.
31. *S.L.S.U.*, pp. 121–49 (248–267).
32. *S.L.S.U.*, pp. 134, 140 (258).

CHAPTER VII

THE KIND OF POET YOU'VE GOT

Between 1935 and the appearance of his *Collected Poems* in 1962, very little poetry by MacDiarmid was published in book form, and nearly all of it is fragmentary. Most of the fragments appear to belong to two colossal poems which have long been on the stocks: *Cornish Heroic Song for Valda Trevlyn* and *Mature Art*. It is possible that they have now merged into one immensely long "poem to end all poems" in MacDiarmid's mind, but more than twenty years ago he seems to have envisaged, and completed, two separate poems. *Mature Art* was to have been published in 1939 by Jack Kahane's Obelisk Press in Paris, but Kahane's death and, later, the War made it impossible to carry out the scheme. An item in the *New Alliance* for March 1940 gives the length of the poem as 20,000 lines, and indicates that it was to be published by subscription.

Early in 1939, the total length of the *Cornish Heroic Song* was stated to be "some 60,000 lines,"[1] and the parts of it that have so far appeared[2] must therefore be regarded as mere bagatelles. Perhaps the "Lament for the Great Music" has become a part of it, along with many other separately-published poems, since its general intention seems to be to suggest a vast panorama of Celtic history and pre-history, centring on Cornwall, Wales, Ireland, and Scotland.

The opening section of the *Heroic Song* was published three times (in 1939, 1943, and 1947) before its inclusion in the *Collected Poems* of 1962, and its date of composition has been given by MacDiarmid as 1936. Despite its several appearances, he has given little indication as to what follows it in the main body of the work itself. In form and sometimes in tone it is a Browningesque dramatic monologue, addressed to the poet's Cornish wife, and in point of fact it seems more complete in itself than many of his other poems.

The principal theme that might be taken to link it with the rest of the vast work is suggested by an image to which Moby Dick associations have been given by adroitly whitewashing a different kind of whale:

> The Celtic genius—Cornwall, Scotland, Ireland,
>   Wales—
> Is to the English Ascendancy, the hideous khaki
>   Empire,
> As the white whale is to the killer whale,
> The white whale displaying in its buccal cavity
> The heavy oily blood-rich tongue which is the
>   killer's especial delight.
> The killer slips his head into the behemoth's mouth
> And rives away part after part of the tongue until
> Nothing remains in the white whale's mouth but a
>   cicatrised stump.
> Yet to-day we laugh gaily and show our healthy red
>   tongues,
> Red rags to John Bull—the Celtic colour flaunting
>   again
> In a world where the ravening sub-fusc more and
>   more
> Prevails. We young Celts arise with quick tongues
>   intact
> Though our elders lie tongueless under the ocean of
>   history. . . .
> The deepest blood-being of the white race crying to
>   England
> "Consummatum Est! Your Imperial Pequod is
>   sunk.". . .)[3]

One of the dangers in separating the above from its immediate context is that it may suggest that the theme is simply political. The political union envisaged by the poet between "Workers' republics in Scotland, Ireland, Wales and Cornwall"[4] is an important part, but still only a part, of his theme. In this connexion, it is useful to remember what MacDiarmid said in his autobiography: "I am . . . interested only in a very subordinate way in the politics of Socialism as a political theory; my real concern with Socialism is as an artist's organised approach to the interdependencies of life."[5]

How far his powers of organisation have been successfully employed in the building of these enormous projects remains to be seen. In the meanwhile one boggles at being given a few pages of a poem said to be 60,000 lines long and then discovering that part of what one has been given is also attributed to a different poem. Nor is it possible to discriminate with much confidence between the samples of poetry in *Lucky Poet* (1943), the "New Poems" of *A Kist of Whistles* (1947)—some of which were considerably newer when they appeared in 1922—and the odd pamphlets, *Dìreadh* (1938) and *Poems of the East-West Synthesis* (1946). Even the 1962 volume of *Collected Poems* sometimes adds to the difficulties. For example, it attributes to *Impavidi Progrediamur*[6] an extract from the first of MacDiarmid's "Dìreadh" poems, until then attributed to the *Cornish Heroic Song*.

What is reasonably certain is that the *Cornish Heroic Song* is concerned with an idea that has obsessed MacDiarmid for many years: briefly, the idea that "the impetus to civilisation was an Ur-Gaelic initiative and that in the Gaelic genius lies the reconciliation of East and West."[7] He has pursued innumerable ramifications of this idea through great masses of reading, three of the key books evidently being *Six Thousand Years of Gaelic Grandeur Unearthed* (L. Albert's 1936 edition of Roger O'Conner's *Chronicles of Eri*), L. A. Waddell's *British Edda* (1930), and

Henri Hubert's *Greatness and Decline of the Celts* (1934). He sees the Celt and the Slav both as being "outside Europe," and in finding an ultimate meeting-place for them in Communism he is at the same time creating the "East-West Synthesis" from which he believes the "new beginning" must develop—the new beginning that had so fired his imagination when reading Spengler, and which made its appearance in the first work signed by Hugh MacDiarmid, in 1922.[8]

This is not by any means the only instance of his earliest work casting light on his latest. It was remarked about "Following Rebecca West in Edinburgh" that it offered us the advance handout as a form of literature. The same is true of *The Kind of Poetry I Want*, a potentially endless sequence of samples to which MacDiarmid declared a halt in 1961, when it appeared in book form, announcing that "this is the first time all the pieces have been brought together, set in their proper sequence, and published as a single poem." That being so, he must have rejected a great many of the pieces that had appeared earlier, including one of the best bits, a fine explanation of the screw stroke in billiards and snooker.[9] Also, he must have radically changed the attitude that had led him to give complete freedom to the radio producer, D. G. Bridson, in determining the choice and sequence of passages for a broadcast of the work in 1960.[10]

It might be objected that, instead of spending so much time in telling us about the kind of poetry he would like to be able to write, MacDiarmid should get down to an attempt at writing it. A sympathetic critic, R. L. C. Lorimer, has suggested that in trying to clarify his own conceptions of it the poet *is* writing it: but this is only valid to a certain extent. MacDiarmid wants a poetry that is "above all, controlled," and "organized to the last degree," but what he does in practice in *The Kind of Poetry I Want* is to list an arbitrary number of individual items, many of them certainly of great interest in themselves, but given a semblance of structural organisation only by a very crude linking device. And is he really writing a poem, or would it not be more accurate to say, as he himself said of the *Annals of the Five Senses*, that he is "designing" a mosaic with pieces taken from his reading?

It may be remembered that, on the occasion mentioned above, MacDiarmid was referring to the prose pieces, not the poetry, in the *Annals*. But in his later work he agrees with Chaim Bialik about the "folly of differentiating between prose and poetry,"[11] and indeed much of his verse consists of prose quotations chopped into shorter lines. If every age gets the poetry it deserves, perhaps there is something appropriate about the poet in our time becoming a sort of sub-editor in an intellectual news agency, spotting the most interesting items and arranging them in unexpected sequences that shock the torpid reader into attention. But surely we are right to protest against, or at least regret, the loss of these subtler qualities in the handling of language that used to make the poet's own words so quotable. And who is the surgeon in

> A poetry like an operating theatre,
> Sparkling with a swift, deft energy,
> Energy quiet and contained and fearfully alert,
> In which the poet exists only as a nurse during an
>   operation,
> Who exists only to have a sponge ready when
>   called for,
> Wads of sterilised cotton wool—nothing else
> Having the smallest meaning for her?[12]

The material MacDiarmid uses is often more interesting than that of any other modern poet. Sometimes it is uniquely fascinating in its appeal simultaneously to the intelligence and to the imagination:

> A poetry like the hope of achieving ere very long
> A tolerable idea of what happens from first to last
> If we bend a piece of wire
> Backwards and forwards until it breaks.[13]

But it is possible to appreciate the wonderful eye that spots such items, and the furiously energetic reading of all kinds of periodicals and books that works in its service, while insisting none the less that what is of crucial importance is not the material used by an artist but the way in which he uses it. And MacDiarmid does his material a serious disservice by presenting it in such a dreary package: "Poetry that never for a moment forgets" such-and-such, "not unaware of" this and that, and "like" ever so many other things.

To the first of his "Dìreadh" poems, MacDiarmid prefixed this statement: "I turn from the poetry of beauty to the poetry of wisdom—of 'wisdom', that is to say, the poetry of moral and intellectual problems, and the emotions they generate."[14] It would be more accurate to say that he turned to the poetry of *information*. The most substantial sample we have been given of this kind of poetry is *In Memoriam James Joyce* (1955), regarding which everyone would agree that it is a fantastically informative work, but only a disciple could call it *wise*. Nor does it generate very much emotion—the common factor in the poetry of beauty and the poetry of wisdom, as indicated in the quotation above.

In Memoriam James Joyce is the first part, in over 6,000 lines, of *Mature Art* (or *A Vision of World Language*, or whatever its final title proves to be). Again, it is helpful to relate it to MacDiarmid's early work, and in particular to those parts of the *Annals* in which he wrestled with the problem of how, as an artist, he could put to use even a fraction of the stimuli that his omnivorous reading habits, together with the modern mass media of communication, constantly supplied to his brain: "There was so much to be read that there was hardly time to think. How could he digest the marvellous, the epoch-making truths which every day put before him! And the still more marvellous lies!"[15]

Even the style of those parts of the *Annals* where he packs one parenthesis inside another, and another, is sometimes reproduced in the Joyce poem. (It has always been present, to a greater or less extent, in his everyday prose.) Its usefulness in suggesting the movement of his mind is undeniable, though it sometimes tends to split the reader's head open as he waits with increasing anxiety for the final, closing bracket that perhaps will *never* come—and then where will he be?

Hopkins wrote a chorus for his unfinished play, *St. Winefred's Well*, which begins as follows:

> How to kéep—is there ány any, is there none
>   such, nowhere known some, bow or brooch
>   or braid or brace, láce, latch or catch or key
>   to keep
> Back beauty, keep it, beauty, beauty, beauty,
>   . . . from vanishing away?[16]

MacDiarmid asks the same question of knowledge, not beauty, and the extended parenthesis between the beginning and the end of his question is filled (on an epic scale) with *factual* charms against the powers of mortality. The kind of poetry he wants is a poetry of fact. And as his mind operates in a continuum of factual information, so his poetry presents blocks of facts and whole housing schemes of quotations. The man may live in a two-roomed cottage; his mind requires much more extensive accommodation.

But the artist in MacDiarmid has a weak sense of architectonics. Privately, amongst friends, he has been known to admit this deficiency with cheerful modesty. In print, however, he has found an ingenious way of making it seem a virtue. Claiming that Wagner and Doughty

"knew that we were coming to another of the quantitative—as against accentual—periods in culture," he goes
on to state:

It is this question of quantity as against accent that dis-
torts to most Scots the nature of our pibrochs of the
great period. These knew no "bar". They were *timeless* music—hence their affiliation with plainsong, with
the neuma. Barred music—accented music—finds its
ultimate form in symphony. Unbarred music—
quantity music—expresses itself in pattern-repetition;
hence the idea that the Celt has no architectonic
power, that his art is confined to niggling involutions
and intricacies—yet the ultimate form here is not
symphony; it is epic.[17]

Since we are coming or have come to a quantitative
period in culture, and the Age of Communism requires
an epic expression "in keeping with the great enter-
prise," pattern-repetition is what we ought to have—not
architectonic power. Presumably it is in some such terms
that MacDiarmid would defend the way in which *In
Memoriam James Joyce* is put together. But the method as
used by him is sometimes so primitive that it grates pain-
fully against the erudite sophistication of his material.
Granted that learned bibliographies are a kind of
pattern-repetition, the question remains whether he
deploys them in his poetry with even that degree of
control that registers the point at which they become
comic. Any list of names may have the appeal of poetry
at its most primitive level, but some names have more
appeal than others, as he himself indicates:

Shirokogoroff's *Psychomental Complex of the Tungus*;
(If that line is not great poetry in itself
Then I don't know what poetry is!)[18]

It is only too rarely that his sense of humour (and sense of
discrimination) is brought into play; usually it is stifled

by a lust for the encyclopedic that insists on packing everything in at any cost to the form. Only this crudest kind of pattern-repetition could encompass so much: "We have of course studied thoroughly . . . And we are fully aware of . . . And on to . . . We are familiar with . . . So we have read . . . And we have read all that is to be read on. . . ." The very boasting in such passages is aimed at attracting the attention of the reader, if only by way of irritation, because the structural device itself is patently incapable of sustaining his interest.

The shift from the singular to the plural of the first person does little to soften the point that it would be better to avoid the first person altogether in deploying material that is not only factual but also conveyed very often in the words, and to some extent the style, of other people. This leads to a further point concerning rhythm. MacDiarmid has not only abandoned the distinction whereby sound-qualities and rhythms are much more highly organised in verse than in prose; he has gone still further in much of this work and discarded the procedure of writing, whether in verse or prose, in a rhythm of his his own choosing. For at least the longer quotations that he uses in his mosaics must obviously retain the rhythm given them by their original authors.

This is not to deny that if one takes a piece of some one else's prose and distributes it in verse-lines, one is con-tributing *something*, rhythmically speaking. The question is "how much?"—and the answer in MacDiarmid's case is "generally far too little for a creative artist." There are exceptions, however, one of the best of which is to be found in the passage about Karl Kraus in the first part of *In Memoriam James Joyce*.

This passage occupies about half-a-dozen pages of the book. It is taken from a long unsigned article in the *Times Literary Supplement* to which MacDiarmid directs the reader in a footnote[19]—an article written by a fine stylist with a very unusual feeling for rhythm. Anyone can

see this, going from MacDiarmid to his original; the
point is that MacDiarmid saw it first, and brought out
the rhythmical pattern of some parts of the prose by
cutting them into verse-lines:

> What was the inspiration of his vast productivity?
> The answer is Hamlet's: 'Words, words, words!',
> And the commas between them
> And the deeds they beget
> And the deeds they leave undone;
> And the word that was at the beginning,
> And, above all, the words that were at the end.[20]

Anyone who looks closely at the little changes, including
word-substitutions, that have been made in the original,
will recognise that the hand of the poet has not lost its old
cunning.

Other examples appear from time to time, as always in
MacDiarmid, even when the prospects seem to be at their
dimmest; and several of these he himself has selected
from *In Memoriam James Joyce* for preservation in the
Collected Poems. Among them is the wonderful interpola-
tion of a piece of scientific information as an analogy at
the point in the Karl Kraus passage where the original
refers to Hölderlin, who "sought, and often miraculously
found, the word with which silence speaks its own silence
without breaking it":

> (Silence supervening at poetry's height,
> Like the haemolytic streptococcus
> In the sore throat preceding rheumatic fever
> But which, at the height of the sickness,
> Is no longer there, but has been and gone!
> Or as 'laughter is the representative of tragedy
> When tragedy is away.')[21]

Not thus preserved by MacDiarmid, but equally fine, is
the factual description of the growth of nerves, muscles,
bones, lungs, and so on, in the foetus—

> A pseudo-aquatic parasite, voiceless as a fish,
> Yet containing within itself an instrument of voice
> Against the time when it *will* talk—

which he suddenly makes analagous to the later work of James Joyce, "vastly outrunning present needs . . . but providing for the developments to come."[22]

To MacDiarmid, Joyce, Doughty, and himself are "harbingers of the epical age of Communism,"[23] when everyone will have followed the directive of Lenin and "worked over in his consciousness the whole inheritance of human knowledge,"[24] using a great deal more than the present average of two per cent or so of his brain cells. Joyce's significance lies especially in developing the resources of language, and we have already seen how *Ulysses* and Jamieson's *Dictionary* were associated in MacDiarmid's mind when he began the experiments that led to his own finest work in Scots. Again, when he turned to "synthetic" English, he said that, except for such experimentalists as Joyce, writers were employing

> only a fraction—and for the most part all the same fraction—of the expressive resources of the language in question. . . . The reason why nineteen-twentieths of any language are never used is shrewdly related to the problem of the freedom of the consciousness. . . . Language is as much a determinant of what is expressed in it as a medium of expression. . . . Theoretically I agree with Joyce in regard to the utilization of a multi-linguistic medium—a synthetic use, not of any particular language, but of all languages.[25]

Thus *In Memoriam James Joyce* has as one of its epigraphs the following remark by Soloviev: "The true unity of language is not an Esperanto or Volapuk or everyone speaking French, not a single language, but an all-embracing language, an interpenetration of all languages." If we substitute "basic English" for "French" in that statement, we arrive at MacDiarmid's principal theme, and see the essential fitness of the title he chose for his book.

In other respects, and especially where structure is concerned, the association with Joyce is unfortunate. But here, with an unexpectedness that one comes to expect, MacDiarmid would link Joyce with Whitman. His favourite quotation from the latter comes from *A Backward Glance O'er Travel'd Roads*: "The true use for the imaginative faculty of modern times is to give ultimate vivification to facts, to science, and to common lives."[26]

In *This Modern Poetry* (1935), Babette Deutsch made use of this quotation, together with others from Thoreau, Frost, and Marianne Moore, in a way that suggests that MacDiarmid's turning towards a "poetry of fact" may have been influenced by her book. Her quotation from Thoreau is particularly suggestive:

I have a commonplace book for facts and another for poetry, but I find it difficult always to preserve the vague distinctions which I had in mind, for the most interesting and beautiful facts are so much the more poetry, and that is their success. . . . I see that if my facts were sufficiently vital and significant—perhaps transmuted more into the substance of the human mind—I should need but one book of poetry to contain them all.[27]

The weakness of MacDiarmid's use of facts is that he is oftener content to catalogue them with Whitman than to follow Thoreau's hint of the need to transmute them imaginatively into "the substance of the human mind." When a fact is just a fact, its discovery in a book may have an emotional effect on us, but it is rarely if ever that we return to the book in order to re-experience the emotion, as we do when fact has been made into good art. And since MacDiarmid is concerned with bridging the gap between science and poetry, it is difficult to see what else he can use but the common factor of emotion. If there is a "rhythm" of ideas, we recognise it because it gives us an emotional satisfaction.

His "poetry of fact" is also unsatisfying because it gives so little scope to the most original part of his formidable mind, its speculative power. It is mainly a poetry of the Fancy, using the term in its Coleridgian sense, not to disparage the work but to indicate its limitation. That is, it is largely the product of "a mode of memory emancipated from the order of time and space, while it is blended with and modified by that empirical phenomenon of the will which we express by the word Choice. But equally with the ordinary memory the Fancy must receive all its materials ready made from the law of association."[28] Nevertheless, it should be added that *In Memoriam James Joyce* does not represent the best of MacDiarmid's later poetry. The extracts he has given us from the still unpublished *Impavidi Progrediamur*[29] suggest that this will prove to be a much superior book.

He writes far too much, he quotes far too much, he discriminates far too little, and his sense of form is weak. But he is a major poet, and there is no book he has written that does not, however partially or intermittently, testify to that fact.

> Surrendering and dispersing his identity
> He yet made the world feel him at last
> As something tough, something singular, something
> leathery with life. . . .

> But there was one virtue the meanest allotment-
> holders have
> Which he conspicuously lacked—they *weed* their
> plots
> While he left to time and chance
> And the near-sighted pecking of critics
> The necessary paring and cutting.[30]

REFERENCES

1. *V. of S.*, Dec. 1938—Feb. 1939, p. 4.
2. *E.g., V. of S.*, Dec. 1938—Feb. 1939, pp. 13–21; *Criterion*, Jan. 1938, pp. 195–203; *K.W.*, pp. 19–24.
3. *K.W.*, p. 22 (379).
4. *L.P.*, p. 26.
5. *L.P.*, p. 241.
6. The second, as yet unpublished, volume of *Mature Art* (or *A Vision of World Language* as it now seems to be called). A few extracts appear in *C.P.*, and other passages have been broadcast on the B.B.C. Third Programme (19 Dec. 1956).
7. *G.T.* (1946 edn.), p. xxiii.
8. See above p. 22.
9. *L.P.*, pp. 131–2.
10. B.B.C. Third Programme, 14 Mar. 1960.
11. *I.M.J.J.*, p. 16.
12. *K.P.W.*, p. 37.
13. *K.P.W.*, p. 21.
14. *V. of S.*, Dec. 1938—Feb. 1939, p. 13.
15. *A.*, p. 110.
16. *Poems* (ed. Bridges), London 1918, p. 54.
17. "Charles Doughty and the Need for Heroic Poetry," in *M.S.*, Jan. 1936, pp. 308–9.
18. *I.M.J.J.*, p. 64.
19. "Satirist in the Modern World," in *T.L.S.*, 8 May 1953, pp. 293–5.
20. *I.M.J.J.*, p. 45.
21. *I.M.J.J.*, p. 47 (410).
22. *I.M.J.J.*, p. 143.
23. *I.M.J.J.*, p. 23.
24. Quoted, *e.g.*, in *L.P.*, p. xxii.
25. *F.M.*, 9 Dec. 1933, p. 11.
26. *Complete Poetry and Prose*, New York 1954, p. 471.
27. *This Modern Poetry*, 1935, p. 33.
28. *Biographia Literaria* (Everyman edn.), p. 146.
29. *E.g., C.P.*, pp. 418–32, and script of radio programme produced by D. G. Bridson, B.B.C. Third Programme, 19 Dec. 1956.
30. *K.W.*, p. 17.

CHAPTER VIII

REPUTATION

MacDiarmid addressed his work in the first place to his fellow countrymen. Since there were no good literary periodicals in Scotland, he had to create his own, and the circulation of these was very small. However, the aims of his *Scottish Chapbook* (1922–3) and its successors were made known to a wider public through the columns of the *Glasgow Herald*, one of the two principal newspapers in the country. On the staff of the *Herald* were William Power, Alexander McGill and Robert Bain, all of whom quickly recognised MacDiarmid's gifts, and as early as 16 May 1922, an item headed "Modern Scottish Verse" shows that the *Herald*'s policy was to give strong support to his new ventures, with poems and prose by him appearing from time to time thereafter.

When MacDiarmid's own periodicals had given up the unequal struggle, McGill saw a new way of reaching potential readers by making use of the *Scottish Educational Journal*, a weekly read mainly by teachers. His article, "Towards a Scottish Renaissance"[1] paved the way for MacDiarmid's highly provocative "Contemporary Scottish Studies" series, which began in June 1925 and led to violent controversies in the columns of the *Journal*. By the time he published the articles in book form the following year, he had become notorious, and it should be noted that opposition to MacDiarmid *as a writer* in Scotland was based much more on these articles than upon his early experiments in verse. The latter were accepted and appreciated by a surprising number of readers, when one remembers the extent of the public for any kind of serious poetry.

MacDiarmid has always delighted in the most out-
rageous sort of self-propaganda, and he carefully con-
solidated his notoriety. *To Circumjack Cencrastus* (1930)
was heralded by advance reviews written anonymously
by the poet himself in at least half a dozen different
journals—"each a different article; quite a little journalistic feat"![2] He was at pains to point out that *Cencrastus*
contained outspoken attacks on "all manner of prominent
Scottish personalities" and that "many of its passages
would be characterised by any section of the Christian
Church as blankly blasphemous."[3] Less predictably, he
also criticised his own "gratuitous ill-will," "Ishmaelit-
ism," "pretentious pedantry," "intellectual arrogance,"
and "cheap sarcasm" with almost as much gusto as he
had shown in criticising other people's failings in the book
itself.[4]

The result was that even his poetry made news in the
Scottish press. The Glasgow *Daily Record* greeted the
appearance of *Cencrastus* with what it called "a double-
barrelled review by two prominent literary figures," the
Rev. Dr Lauchlan Maclean Watt (who was side-swiped
in the poem) and William Power.[5] Enraged letters to the
Editor followed.

His fame, as distinct from his notoriety, also grew
steadily until the series of crises that took him to the
Shetland Islands and away from the public arena. When
he protested against a very unfavourable anonymous
review of *Scots Unbound* (1932) in a journal edited by his
friend Power,[6] the reviewer roundly declared that "there
is no important Scottish writer to-day, critical or
creative, but has praised MacDiarmid's poetry, and no
other Scottish writer has received such attention or been
discussed so much. . . . Martyrdom has eluded him. He
is a successful poet." But the successful poet, only a few
months later, was struggling in exile against abject
poverty and physical hardship, with his wife and their
baby.

During the years in the Shetlands comparatively little was heard of MacDiarmid as a poet, and the general assumption was that his vein of poetry had been more or less exhausted. In a contribution to *Edinburgh Essays in Scots Literature* (1933)[7] Ian Gordon voiced the majority opinion by describing him as "the finest lyric poet in Scotland" but deploring his recent change to "a style that is inconsequent always, incoherent very often, and is all too seldom poetry." Of more consequence were the reservations expressed by a long-time admirer, Edwin Muir, whose judgment could be expected to have effects outside of Scotland.

Muir had written the first important criticism of MacDiarmid's work ever to appear, a review of *Annals of the Five Senses* for Orage's *New Age*.[8] Some remarks about the un-Englishness of the author led to a comparison with Joyce, and Muir gave it as his opinion that "except Mr. Joyce, nobody at present is writing more resourceful English prose." Again, in reviewing *Sangschaw* and introducing the Scottish literary movement to American readers in the *Saturday Review of Literature*, he was at pains to emphasise the un-Englishness of MacDiarmid's work, and not only in the obvious matter of language: "This vision is profoundly alien to the spirit of English poetry. ... It is the product of a realistic, or more exactly a materialistic, imagination, which seizing upon everyday reality shows not the strange beauty which that sometimes takes on, but rather the beauty which it possesses normally and in use." Comparing MacDiarmid with his English contemporaries, "in curious speculation and half-fantastic thought he is certainly as original as Mr. Graves; his descriptions are more economical and, I think, more vivid than Mr. Blunden's, and his mysticism more organic with his general mood than Mr. de la Mare's."[9]

Cencrastus had been for Muir "a literary event of capital importance, and a work of great brilliance and power,"[10] but by 1934 he was expressing grave doubts about the possibilities of Scots as a literary medium.[11] Then he seemed to have swallowed his doubts when in May 1935 he wrote that MacDiarmid "has done something for Scottish poetry of quite unique value; he has made it a vehicle capable of expressing, like English or French, the feelings and thoughts of the contemporary world."[12] A year later, however, he wrote an article for *Outlook* setting out his case against the use of Scots,[13] and this became a central point in his book, *Scott and Scotland* (1936). Remarking that Scotland has lacked a homogenous language since the sixteenth century, he said that the predicament of the Scottish writer

> cannot be solved by writing poems in Scots, or by looking forward to some hypothetical Scotland in the future. . . . Scottish poetry exists in a vacuum. . . . Hugh MacDiarmid has recently tried to revive it by impregnating it with all the contemporary influences of Europe one after another, and thus galvanise it into life by a series of violent shocks. In carrying out this experiment he has written some remarkable poetry; but he has left Scottish verse very much where it was before.[14]

Splinters from the ensuing explosion are to be found in many of MacDiarmid's later writings. To adapt a celebrated MacDiarmidism, from being a man after Edwin Muir's heart he became a man after Edwin Muir's blood, and though Muir subsequently modified his views to some extent, the breach between them was never healed. It should be noted, however, that MacDiarmid was not concerned directly with himself, but with the implication that it would be a waste of time for *other* writers to continue the attempt at reviving Scots as a literary language.

When the War brought him back to Clydeside, a group of young writers quickly formed round him, most of them

writing verse in Scots or Gaelic, for which they found an
enthusiastic publisher in William Maclellan of Glasgow.
The greatness of MacDiarmid's own work in Scots was
now widely recognised in Scottish literary circles, and he
was in some danger of becoming a national monument.
The danger was not so great where Muir was concerned,
however. In the latter's study of *The Present Age From
1914*, he said that he would make no attempt to deal with
contemporary Scottish literature, but he did in fact deal
briefly with MacDiarmid's work, which he compared
with that of MacDiarmid's arch-enemy, Roy Campbell:
"Technically Campbell is by far the more accomplished
poet, but MacDiarmid excels him in intelligence and in
grotesque, satirical fancy, half-philosophical, half comic."
Of *A Drunk Man* he observed that "technically it is
uneven and often careless, but it contains brilliant passages, it is seldom flat, and it is the work of an interesting
mind. MacDiarmid's later poetry, much of it Com-
munistic, is poor by comparison and often dull."[15]

The later work, of which *In Memoriam James Joyce* is the
principal example, has not added much to his reputation
in Scotland, though two of his most perceptive critics,
David Daiches and Edwin Morgan, have argued per-
suasively on its behalf.[16] Morgan's principal contribution
in this respect appeared in the *Festschrift* published in
Edinburgh to celebrate MacDiarmid's seventieth birthday in August 1962. As might be expected of such a
publication, the *Festschrift* has its ups and downs, but it
contains some excellent articles and shows how enormously stimulating the man and his work have been to
Scotsmen of different generations. It would have had a
wider impact, however, if its editors had obtained contributions from more than one writer not directly connected
with Scotland.

The poverty of Scottish literary life is clear enough
from the fact that only two reviews of any consequence
greeted the belated publication of MacDiarmid's *Collected*

Poems in Scotland, after Macmillan of New York had brought the book out there. In the *Scotsman*, a newspaper which for many years did not so much as mention MacDiarmid's name, Andrew Hood declared that "this collection shows conclusively that he is a poet of the first rank," and "it is time that Scotland, and not merely a few percipient Scots, recognised his stature."[17] Less ironically, he was acknowledged by Edwin Morgan in the *Glasgow Herald* to be

> a man who has extended not only Scottish poetry but our consciousness of the conditions of existence in a new and convincing way. It seems to me that MacDiarmid has little to fear from comparison with those who could be thought of as his most distinguished contemporaries: yet when will we see English criticism recognising the fact? What he may lose to T. S. Eliot in fastidious precision of language or to Ezra Pound in music and cadence, he gains in the greater interest of his subject-matter. . . . What he loses to Wallace Stevens in brilliance of metaphor and symbol he gains by command of simile and analogy. Why then has he not achieved the estimation these poets have achieved?[18]

One reason is the stubborn English prejudice against the use of Scots *as such*. Even in anglicised Scotland there is a sufficient minimum of good will which leads a certain number of people to do their homework before coming to a decision about the value of MacDiarmid's verse in Scots. But in England it is only too clear that he "ought" to write in English. Therefore not one English critic of considerable influence had printed a good word about that great poem *A Drunk Man Looks At The Thistle* (1926) prior to its reappearance in the *Collected Poems* thirty-six years later. F. R. Leavis was able to praise the "Second Hymn to Lenin" in a volume where all the other poems were written, or turned into, "standard" English; and Cecil Day Lewis could affirm the importance to the

literary historian of the "First Hymn," which made its
initial appearance in Lascelles Abercrombie's *New English
Poems*: but even in the latter case we have John Lehmann's protest that "considering the barrier that the
Scots vernacular forms for most Southern Englishmen, it
is unlikely that MacDiarmid's actual influence can have
been more than slight."[19]

The publication of the *Collected Poems* compelled English critics to give serious consideration to MacDiarmid's
early work in Scots nearly forty years after it was written.
One wonders how *The Waste Land* would have fared in
similar circumstances. But of course it would never be
necessary for the sympathetic critic to shield Eliot from
"the non-Scots reader" who might be expected to say:
"Not merely is the subject barbarously provincial, but
enclosed within the barbed-wire of dialect."[20]

"To celebrate his seventieth birthday the adulation,
no doubt, will flow in,"[21] said A. Alvarez in the London
Observer, where MacDiarmid attained fame at last in a
"Profile" containing the following statements: "His
father was a postman and his mother the daughter of an
agricultural labourer. He has never tried to deny these
roots; he still, for example, smokes an ounce of thick
black tobacco every day."[22] But it is not an easy matter in
England to catch up with MacDiarmid so as even to
praise him significantly. Thus, a basically sympathetic
review by Donald Davie in the *New Statesman* was
weakened by a tendentious linking of MacDiarmid to
English writers, his early lyrics being associated with
Hardy, and "Dìreadh III" with, of all things, Wordsworth's lines "When to the Attractions of the Busy
World."[23] It was agreeable to see the *Collected Poems* so
favourably reviewed, but the best criticism of MacDiarmid to have appeared in England has not been by
English writers but by Burns Singer (in 1957)[24] and by
the author of an article, "Revival of the Scottish Language," in the *Times Literary Supplement* of 8 Jan. 1954.

In the United States, nothing of critical importance appeared between Muir's review of *Sangschaw* in 1925 and Babette Deutsch's book *This Modern Poetry* in 1935. The first really substantial consideration of MacDiarmid's work was an article in the *Sewanee Review* by James G. Southworth, reprinted as a chapter of his book on modern British poetry, *Sowing the Spring* (1940).[25] As in England, the language difficulty loomed much larger than it need have done, though Southworth was sympathetic towards most of MacDiarmid's aims and impressed by his powers as a thinker. It took a Scottish critic, David Daiches, to make the essential point that "MacDiarmid does not use Scots as an *alternative* to English; he uses it for effects which are *unobtainable* in English"—as also to make American readers aware of the hard facts behind the rhetoric of MacDiarmid's nationalism: "All informed and disinterested observers of the Scottish scene agree that Scotland's position has for centuries been comparable to that of the South after the Civil War."[26]

Daiches' excellent article in *Poetry* (Chicago) appeared in 1948. Twelve years elapsed before an American critic, M. L. Rosenthal, could say with assurance that MacDiarmid's best work is in Scots and show that he had the necessary "sympathetic ear" for what he called a "half-foreign tongue."[27] All the more credit, therefore, to the New York publishers who brought out the *Collected Poems*. Louise Bogan reviewed this book for the *New Yorker* without revealing what had led her to risk her critical reputation with the judgment that "the early poems, chiefly lyrical, have great charm, in spite of the fact that they are written for the most part in a mixture of Scottish dialects."[28] The New York *Times* consulted Daiches, who said: "Our gratitude goes out to Macmillan for producing this first collected edition of one of the very great poets of our time."[29]

Elsewhere, MacDiarmid's reputation has been too

devious to trace except in the most summary form here.
Denis Saurat introduced him to French readers in 1924,
in an essay which embodied translations of half a dozen
of the earliest lyrics in Scots, part of "A Moment in
Eternity" and a sonnet in English. Saurat's version of
"The Watergaw" leaves something to be desired
("Comme il avait plu, par un soir de toute / Je vis une
rare chose," etc.) but he said that this poem in particular
was "un véritable chef d'œuvre . . . de simplicité et de
concision essentielles. . . . Si beaucoup de poèmes de
cette force nous sont révélés, le groupe de la *Renaissance
écossaise* aura tenu sa gageure et conquis une place en
Europe."[30]

Another article by Saurat appeared shortly afterwards
in the *Northern Review*, and this was used again in
Marsyas, a Provençal magazine founded by Sully André
Peyre, to which Saurat contributed under the name of
"Lucilius." He stressed the point that MacDiarmid was
potentially of *European* stature and in this respect should
take the place of Burns: "Burns n'était curopéen que par
ses platitudes."[31] There have been in France at least two
academic theses on MacDiarmid's work as a whole, but
the only substantial book review appears to have been
Michel Habart's of *In Memoriam James Joyce* in *Critique*.[32]

Some of the early Scots lyrics were translated into
Danish by Carl Kjersmeir for his anthology *Liv Og
Legende*, and early in 1926 the Icelandic magazine
Eimreiðin published a long article on the literary move-
ment headed by MacDiarmid.[33] In Ireland, Oliver St
John Gogarty reviewed *A Drunk Man* for the *Irish
Statesman*, saying that this was "the most virile and vivid
poetry written in English or any dialect thereof for many
a long day."[34] The high point of the *Drunk Man* for
Gogarty was the now famous lyric "O Wha's Been Here
Afore Me, Lass," which he showed to Yeats, with the
result that the latter included it in his *Oxford Book of
Modern English Verse*. Gogarty has said that Yeats at that

time was "amazed that there should be such writing and he unaware of it."[35] (MacDiarmid is fond of quoting from friendly and encouraging letters received from Yeats, Eliot, and Dylan Thomas. None of these writers has actually published anything about his work.)

In Germany, there has been a general survey of "Die Schottische Renaissancebewegung"[36] by Reinald Hoops, in 1933, and at least one academic dissertation[37] dealing principally with MacDiarmid, in 1958. Behind the Iron Curtain, where he has travelled widely in recent years, there is reported to be an extensive amount of material. The only example available to the present writer is an article in Polish by George Bidwell, published in 1956.[38] It is unoriginal, and postpones to the future, as he himself does, the necessary reconciliation between the immense intellectual snobbery to which MacDiarmid freely admits[39] and his nevertheless genuine feeling that "the working-class have always stood, and will always stand, in the relation to me not of 'they' but of 'we'."[40] This should keep the dialecticians busy for quite some time to come.

REFERENCES

1. *S.E.J.*, 16 Jan. 1925, p. 66.
2. Letter from MacDiarmid to Miss Helen B. Cruickshank, 10 Oct. 1930.
3. "A Poet Runs Amok," in *D.R.*, 24 Sep. 1930.
4. "Ptelon," "Blasphemy and Divine Philosophy Mixed," in *S.O.*, 2 Oct. 1930, p. 12.
5. "Two Views of Hugh MacDiarmid's New Poem," in *D.R.*, 29 Oct. 1930.
6. "The Present Work of Hugh MacDiarmid," in

S.O., 22 Dec. 1932, p. 11. See also various letters in *S.O.*, 7, 14, 21 Jan. 1933.
7. "Modern Scots Poetry," in *Edinburgh Essays on Scots Literature*, Edinburgh, 1933, pp. 126–48.
8. "Readers and Writers," in *N.A.*, 15 Nov. 1923, pp. 32–3.
9. "The Scottish Renaissance," in *Saturday Review of Literature*, 31 Oct. 1925, p. 259.
10. "Scottish Letters in 1931," in *S.O.*, 17 Dec. 1931, p. 15.

11. "Literature in Scotland," in *Spectator*, 25 May 1934, p. 823.

12. "Literature from 1910 to 1935," *Scotsman*, 6 May 1935.

13. "A Literature Without a Language," in *Outlook*, Jun. 1936.

14. *Scott and Scotland*, London 1936, pp. 19, 20, 21–2.

15. *The Present Age from 1914*, London 1939, pp. 115–16.

16. D. Daiches, "MacDiarmid's New Poem," in *Lines Review*, Aug. 1955, pp. 22–6. E. Morgan, "Jujitsu for the Educated," in *Twentieth Century*, Sep. 1956, pp. 223–31; and "Poetry and Knowledge in MacDiarmid's Later Work," in *Festschrift*, Edinburgh 1962, pp. 129–39.

17. "A Unique Scots Poet," in *Scotsman*, 11 Aug. 1962.

18. "Hugh MacDiarmid: The Poet at Seventy," in *Glasgow Herald*, 11 Aug. 1962.

19. F. R. Leavis, "Hugh MacDiarmid—Second Hymn to Lenin," in *Scrutiny*, Dec. 1935, p. 305. C. Day Lewis, *A Hope for Poetry*, Oxford 1934, pp. 51, 53. John Lehmann, "Some Revolutionary Trends in English Poetry 1930–1935," *International Literature* (Moscow) Apr. 1936, pp. 60–9.

20. John Montague, "International Thistle," in *Spectator*, 17 Aug. 1962. (The point of view is not Montague's but that of the reader over his shoulder.)

21. A. Alvarez, "Dialect and the Dialectic," in *Observer*, 12 Aug. 1962.

22. "The Poet of the Gaelic World," in *Observer*, 12 Aug. 1962.

23. Donald Davie, "A'e Golden Lyric," in *New Statesman*, 10 Aug. 1962.

24. Burns Singer, "Scarlet Eminence," in *Encounter*, Mar. 1957, pp. 49–62.

25. "Hugh MacDiarmid," in *Sewanee Review*, Jan.–Mar. 1940, pp. 105–18; *Sowing the Spring*, Oxford 1940, pp. 92–107.

26. David Daiches, "Hugh MacDiarmid and Scottish Poetry," in *Poetry* (Chicago), Jul. 1948, pp. 202–18.

27. M. L. Rosenthal, *The Modern Poets*, New York 1960, pp. 131–6.

28. *New Yorker*, 17 Nov. 1962.

29. *Times* (N.Y.), 25 Feb. 1962.

30. "Le Groupe de 'La Renaissance écossaise'," in *R.A.*, Apr. 1924, pp. 295–307.

31. "La Renaissance écossaise," in *N.R.*, Jun.–Jul. 1924, pp. 116–17. See also *Marsyas*, Sep. 1924.

32. Michel Habart, "Hugh MacDiarmid: Visionnaire du language," in *Critique*, Dec. 1955, pp. 1056–63.

33. Alex. McGill, "Bokmentavakningin skozka," in

Eimreiðin, Jan.–Mar. 1926, pp. 20–35.

34. "Literature and Life," in *Irish Statesman*, 8 Jan. 1927, pp. 431–3.

35. Letter to the author, 4 Sep. 1951.

36. *Englische Studien*, 67, Heft 3, 1933, pp. 371–90.

37. Rolf Blaeser, "New Scots Renascence," Inaugural- Dissertation zur Erlangung des Doktorgrades der Philosophischen Fakultät der Johann— — Wolfgang — Goethe — Universität Frankfurt. Dillinger/Saar, 1958.

38. "MacDiarmid," *Tworczość*, Summer 1956, pp. 202–4.

39. *L.P.*, p. 78.

40. *L.P.*, p. 231–2.

SELECT BIBLIOGRAPHY

I. HUGH MACDIARMID (C. M. GRIEVE)

1. Verse

Sangschaw. Edinburgh (Blackwood) 1925.

Penny Wheep. Edinburgh (Blackwood) 1926.

A Drunk Man Looks at the Thistle. Edinburgh (Blackwood) 1926. New
    edn., Glasgow (Caledonian Press) 1953. Third edn. Edinburgh
    (Castle Wynd Printers) 1956; reissued 1962.

To Circumjack Cencrastus. Edinburgh (Blackwood) 1930.

First Hymn to Lenin and Other Poems. London (Unicorn Press) 1931.

Scots Unbound and Other Poems. Stirling (Mackay) 1932.

Stony Limits and Other Poems. London (Gollanz) 1934.

Selected Poems. London (Macmillan) 1934.

Second Hymn to Lenin and Other Poems. London (Nott) 1935.

Selected Poems, ed. R. Crombie Saunders. Glasgow (W. Maclellan)
    [1944].

Speaking for Scotland. Baltimore (Contemporary Poetry) 1946.

A Kist of Whistles. Glasgow (W. Maclellan) [1947].

In Memoriam James Joyce. Glasgow (W. Maclellan) 1955.

Stony Limits and Scots Unbound and Other Poems. Edinburgh (Castle
    Wynd Printers) 1956.

Three Hymns to Lenin. Edinburgh (Castle Wynd Printers) 1957.

The Battle Continues. Edinburgh (Castle Wynd Printers) 1957.

The Kind of Poetry I Want. Edinburgh (K. D. Duval) 1961.

Collected Poems. New York (Macmillan) and Edinburgh (Oliver &
    Boyd) 1962.

2. Prose

Contemporary Scottish Studies. London (L. Parsons) 1926.

Albyn, or Scotland and the Future. London (K. Paul) 1927.

At the Sign of the Thistle. London (S. Nott) [1934].

Scottish Eccentrics. London (G. Routledge) 1936.

The Islands of Scotland. London (Batsford) 1939.

Lucky Poet. London (Methuen) 1943.

Cunninghame Graham: A Centenary Study. Glasgow (Caledonian Press)
    [1952].

Francis George Scott: An Essay. Edinburgh (M. Macdonald) 1955.

Burns Today and Tomorrow. Edinburgh (Castle Wynd Printers) 1959.

3. Verse and Prose

Annals of the Five Senses. Montrose (C. M. Grieve) 1923; Edinburgh (Porpoise Press) 1930.

Scottish Scene (with Lewis Grassic Gibbon). London (Jarrolds) 1934.

4. Pamphlets

The Present Condition of Scottish Arts and Affairs. [n.p. or d.— 1927?]. (P.E.N. Club).

The Present Position of Scottish Music. Montrose (C. M. Grieve) 1927.

The Lucky Bag. Edinburgh (Porpoise Press) 1927. (Poems)

The Scottish National Association of April Fools. Aberdeen (The University Press) 1928.

Second Hymn to Lenin. Thakeham (Valda Trevlyn) [1932].

Tarras. Edinburgh(*Free Man*) 1932. (Poem.)

Five Bits of Miller. London(The Author) 1934.

Scotland in 1980. Montrose (The Author) [1935].

Charles Doughty and the Need for Heroic Poetry. [St Andrews 1936.]

Dìreadh. [Dunfermline (*Voice of Scotland*)1938.] (Poem.)

Cornish Heroic Song for Valda Trevlyn. Glasgow (Caledonian Press) [1943].

Poems of the East-West Synthesis. Glasgow (Caledonian Press) 1946.

Fidelity in Small Things. [n.p. or d.] (J. W. Sault).

David Hume, Scotland's Greatest Son. Edinburgh (Paperback Bookshop) [1962].

The Man of (Almost) Independent Mind. Edinburgh (Giles Gordon) 1962.

Bracken Hills in Autumn. Edinburgh (C. H. Hamilton) 1962. (Poem.)

The Ugly Birds Without Wings. Edinburgh (Allan Donaldson) 1962.

5. Translations

The Handmaid of the Lord. Translation of Ramon Maria de Tenreiro: *La Esclava del Señor.* London (Secker) 1930.

The Birlinn of Clanranald. Translation of Alexander MacDonald: *Birlinn Chlann-Raghnaill.* St Andrews (Abbey Bookshop) 1935.

Aniara (with Elspeth Harley Schubert). Translation of Harry Martinson: *Aniara.* London (Hutchinson) 1962.

6. Editorial Work

Northern Numbers [First Series]. Edinburgh (T. N. Foulis) 1920.

Northern Numbers. Second Series. Edinburgh (T. N. Foulis) 1921.

Northern Numbers. Third Series. Montrose (C. M. Grieve) 1922.

Robert Burns, 1759–1796. London (E. Benn) 1926.

Living Scottish Poets. London (E. Benn) [1931].

The Golden Treasury of Scottish Poetry. London (Macmillan) 1940.

William Soutar: Collected Poems. London (A. Dakers) 1940.

Selections from the Poems of William Dunbar. Edinburgh (Oliver & Boyd) 1952.

II. OTHERS

1. Collected Criticism

Hugh MacDiarmid: A Festschrift. Edd. K. D. Duval and Sydney Goodsir Smith. Edinburgh (K. D. Duval) 1962.

2. Single Items

AITKEN, MARY BAIRD: "The Poetry of Hugh MacDiarmid," in *Scottish Art and Letters*, No. 4 [1949], pp. 5–25.

CRAIG, DAVID: "Hugh MacDiarmid's Poetry," in *Voice of Scotland*, Apr. 1956, pp. 6–19.

DAICHES, DAVID: "Hugh MacDiarmid and Scottish Poetry," in *Poetry* (Chicago), Jul. 1948, pp. 202–18.

——: "Introduction" to *A Drunk Man Looks at the Thistle*, Glasgow 1953 (and subsequent edns.).

——: "MacDiarmid's New Poem," in *Lines Review*, Aug. 1955, pp. 22–6.

DEUTSCH, BABETTE: *Poetry in Our Time*, New York 1952.

FROST, A. C.: "Hugh MacDiarmid: Scotland's Vortex Maker," in *Bookman*, Sep. 1934, pp. 287–8.

LEAVIS, F. R.: "Hugh MacDiarmid—Second Hymn to Lenin," in *Scrutiny*, Dec. 1935, p. 305.

LINDSAY, MAURICE: *The Scottish Renaissance*, Edinburgh 1948.

MORGAN, EDWIN: "Jujitsu for the Educated," in *Twentieth Century*, Sep. 1956, pp. 223–31.

MUIR, EDWIN: "Readers and Critics," in *New Age*, 15 Nov. 1923, pp. 32–3.

——: "The Scottish Renaissance," in *Saturday Review of Literature*, 31 Oct. 192, p. 259.

——: *Scott and Scotland*, London 1936.

——: *The Present Age from 1914*, London 1937.

"Revival of the Scottish Language," in *Times Literary Supplement*, 8 Jan. 1954, p. 29.

ROSENTHAL, M. L.: *The Modern Poets*, New York 1960.

SAUNDERS, R. CROMBIE: "The Thistle in the Lions Mouth," in *Life and Letters To-day*, Mar. 1945, pp. 147–55.

SINGER, BURNS: "Scarlet Eminence," in *Encounter*, Mar. 1957, pp. 49–62.

SOUTAR, WILLIAM: "The Poetry of Hugh MacDiarmid," in *The Free Man*, 7 Apr. 1934, pp. 8–9.

TINDALL, WILLIAM YORK: *Forces in Modern British Literature, 1885–1946*, New York 1947.

WITTIG, KURT: *The Scottish Tradition in Literature*, Edinburgh 1958.